MONROE COLLEGE LIBRARY

3 73   135 7

D1263866

25,968

TO KILL OR NOT TO KILL

Thoughts on Capital

Punishment

Great Issues of the Day
Number Four
ISSN 0270-7497

Rep. William L. Clay, Sr.
Democrat—First District of Missouri

TO KILL OR NOT TO KILL

Thoughts on Capital Punishment

*Great Issues of the Day
Number Four*

Edited by Michael and Mary Burgess

R. REGINALD
The Borgo Press
San Bernardino, California □ MCMXC

Library of Congress Cataloging-in-Publication Data

Clay, William L.
    To kill or not to kill : thoughts on capital punishment / by Rep.
William L. Clay, Sr. ; edited by Michael and Mary Burgess.
        p. cm. — (Great issues of the day, ISSN 0270-7497 ; no. 4)
    Bibliography: p.
    Includes index.
    ISBN 0-89370-331-1 : $24.95. — ISBN 0-89370-431-8 (pbk.) :
$14.95
        1. Capital punishment—United States. 2. Capital punishment—Re-
ligious aspects—Christianity. I. Title. II. Series.
HV8699.U5C42 1990   87-812
241'.697—dc19   CIP

Copyright © 1990 by William L. Clay, Sr.
All rights reserved. No part of this book may be reproduced in any form
without the expressed written consent of the publisher. Published by arrangement with the author. Printed in the United States of America

Produced, designed, and published by Robert Reginald and Mary A.
Burgess, The Borgo Press, P.O. Box 2845, San Bernardino, CA 92406,
USA. Cover design by Highpoint Type & Graphics, Claremont, CA.
Cover and title page photographs courtesy of Rep. William L. Clay, Sr.

FIRST EDITION——October, 1990

CONTENTS

To my wife Carol,
For her love and friendship,

and

To my children, Vickie, Lacy, Michele,
For patience and understanding

INTRODUCTION

The Question of Capital Punishment

Serious discussion of capital punishment in the United States has, for all practical purposes, been largely confined to scholars, theologians, politicians, and the legal profession. Such forums, both oral and written, have often eluded everyday concerns facing a majority of the public. Perhaps this accounts for recent poll results which show that most Americans favor capital punishment; yet many have never asked themselves the pertinent question, "Why?"

This book is written to prompt those holding such views to at least re-examine the reasons for their positions. Capital punishment, in the context both of Christian ethics and of humanistic logic, poses dilemmas for those who justify it based upon erroneous interpretations of the Bible. It's a mockery of Christian religious principles to pretend that one may selectively break the mandate of the Sixth Commandment—"thou shall not kill"—to justify state executions. Until *all* those who murder in cold blood are treated the same, selectively executing some is a farce.

Historically, race and economic status have been the dominant factors in determining who will or will not be executed in the United States. Few "rich" persons, if any, have ever gone to the gallows. The ranks of the condemned are heavily populated by poor whites—those condemned for reasons other than their specific crimes—and by minorities who are damned by socio-economic pressures. There is only an occasional sprinkling of representatives from the middle class on death row, and none at all from the wealthier segments of society.

In this book, Bill Clay draws on evidence from many different scholarly studies to substantiate charges that the death penalty is never meted out to the economically elite, and that the severity of the punishment received by a criminal is often directly related to the race of both the perpetrator and his victim. A white criminal who abuses a Black victim, or a Black criminal who abuses a Black victim, invariably receive a minimal sentence acceptable under the law, except where a particular crime has become a *cause célèbre*. But Black criminals whose victims are white, or white criminals who prey on white populations, are much more likely to be considered serious threats to an orderly society—and punished accordingly.

Since the Ninety-Seventh Congress, the subject of capital punishment has been a matter of grave concern to members of the Senate and House of Representatives. In 1981 Senators Strom Thurmond of South Carolina and Dennis DeConcini of Arizona introduced a bill to re-establish the death penalty for persons convicted of certain federal crimes. Senator Thurmond is notorious for having led southern Democrats out of the 1948 Democratic Convention (and ultimately out of the Democratic Party) in that year's presidential elections.

William L. Clay, Sr., a ten-term Democratic Congressman representing the First District of Missouri, here addresses the serious questions concerning popularly-held notions about state-approved executions. Without attempting to conceal his personal bias against capital punishment, Clay manages to uncover the many religious inconsistencies confronting a society which overwhelmingly professes to believe in the teachings of Jesus Christ, while simultaneously upholding in almost equal numbers the duty of the government to execute criminals.

His facts have been gleaned from careful readings of works by the foremost authorities in the field of criminal justice and Christian theology. He approaches the subject by scrutinizing the conflict between avowed Christian moral fabric and the reality of Christian behavior.

Clay has a total and unwavering commitment to respect all human life, even the lives of those who are social and political outcasts. His verbal bluntness and polemic style are guaranteed to offend supporters of capital punishment, as well as anti-abortionists and political conservatives.

His style is deliberately provocative, and will undoubtedly raise questions in the minds of those who believe in the right and duty of the state to levy the ultimate punishment. This is Representative Clay's first book—I predict it won't be his last.

—Gwen Giles, Assessor*
City of Saint Louis
October, 1985

*Ms. Giles died in Saint Louis shortly after this introduction was written, in March of 1986.

FOREWORD

The Moral Dilemma of State-Sponsored Murder

The drive to abolish the death penalty is as old as capital punishment itself. Despite widespread support for the death penalty in the United States, critics of the system share the view so aptly expressed by the late Andrei Sakharov:

> I regard the death penalty as a savage and immoral institution...A state, in the person of its functionaries...that takes upon itself the right to the most terrible and irreversible act—the deprivation of life, such a state cannot expect an improvement in the moral atmosphere of its country.

Despite the passage of an historic United Nations resolution advocating the curtailment and eventual abolition of capital punishment, over 125 nations throughout the world continue to exact the ultimate penalty, including Iran, Iraq, Pakistan, Nigeria, South Africa, the Soviet Union, and, sadly, the United States. Interestingly, according to statistics published by Interpol (the International Criminal Police organization), most countries which have abolished the death penalty now boast of lower rates of murder or attempted murder than the so-called "civilized" nations which still employ capital punishment. Perhaps this should tell us something about what really constitutes civilization.

Advocates of capital punishment base their support, in large part, on several popular misconceptions. First, that the death penalty serves as a deterrent to murder. Wrong. In practice, three-fourths of all murders involve family members or close acquaintances who are killed out of anger or passion. Clearly, the threat of execution has little or no effect on such spontaneous, unpremeditated acts. Moreover, most premeditated murders are committed by people who clearly do not expect to be apprehended, and who will state so when and if they are captured. They are thus no more deterred by the death penalty than they would be by life imprisonment or thumb-screws or any other punishment. Finally, it is impossible to demonstrate that capital punishment has any appreciable effect upon the commission of violent crime. In fact, many recent studies suggest that such acts often increase during periods of state-sponsored killings.

Secondly, execution is less expensive than life imprisonment. Wrong again. Capital punishment is far more costly. As Richard McGee, former administrator of the California Correctional System, points out:

> The actual costs of execution, the cost of operating the super-maximum-security condemned unit, the years spent by some inmates in condemned status, and a pro-rata share of top-level prison officials' time spent in administering such units, add up to a cost substantially greater than the cost to retain them in prison the rest of their lives.

Thirdly, only the guilty are executed. Still wrong. In New Jersey in 1918, George Brandon was executed for a murder which another man confessed to months later. Frank Smith was executed in Connecticut in 1949, only to be proven innocent minutes after his death. In 1963, Florida condemned two men, Freddie Pitts and Wilbert Lee, to the electric chair; in 1975 their sentences were overturned, and they were fortunately released after having served twelve years in prison. In this regard, Harry W. Fogle, Chief Judge of the Sixth Judicial Circuit, Florida, reflected:

> In my own experience, I know of four persons convicted of first-degree murder and sentenced to death who were later found to be innocent...Prosecutors and legislators are fond of saying that our seemingly interminable appellate processes are a guarantee against error. The cases of which I speak were not corrected through appellate processes, but through confession of the ones actually guilty, long after the appellate processes had been exhausted.

Fourthly, capital punishment is equitably administered. Once again, wrong. The death penalty is overwhelmingly imposed on the poorer segments of society, including minorities. Typically, death row inmates were too poor and too ignorant to retain competent and experienced counsel, but were instead assigned young, inexperienced public defenders. Obviously, expensive private attorneys who specialize in criminal law are far more likely to win reduced prison sentences, favorable plea bargaining agreements, or outright acquittal for their equally guilty clients. As for race, every major study of the imposition of capital punishment indicates that the color of one's skin plays a prominent role in one's chances of actually facing the ultimate punishment. A vastly disproportionate percentage of Black citizens are sentenced to death, particularly if the victim is white. In North Carolina, for example, Blacks constitute less than 25 percent of the population, but account for 70.5 percent of all death sentences levied in the state since 1910; 78 percent of those actually executed in North Carolina in the twentieth century have been black. Furthermore, 57 percent of all Blacks sentenced to death have been executed, while only 40 percent of whites on death row have gone to the gallows. This has led former U.S. Supreme Court justice William O. Douglas to observe:

> The discretion of judges and juries in imposing the death penalty enables the penalty to be selectively applied, feeding prejudices against the accused if he is poor and despised, and lacking political clout, or if he is a member of a suspect and unpopular minority, and saving those who, by social position, may be in a more protected position.

The arguments against capital punishment are many and varied. Major objections include: the cruelty of death row; discrimination in the imposition of the death penalty; capriciousness of indictments and prosecutions; possibility of error; inadequacy of legal representation for the poor; inequity of state clemency laws; and the unfairness of jury selection in death penalty cases. Perhaps this is why Lewis Lawes, who, as the former warden of Sing Sing Prison in New York, escorted 150 men and women to their deaths, was moved to remark: "Not only does capital punishment fail in its justification, but no punishment could be invented with so many inherent defects."

To Kill or Not To Kill is a remarkable book. Indeed, Representative William L. Clay, Sr., seizes the opportunity to explode the comfortable myths which society has adopted to justify killing those poor unfortunates who, for a variety of reasons, have violated its fundamental rules. In many ways, this work is a frontal assault on the very assumptions of our entire legal system. Clay's book deserves the widest possible audience; its vision and humanity mesh to produce a volume of singular importance—one that promises to spark a badly-needed reassessment of the capital punishment controversy. For those naysayers who continue to cling comfortably to the sundry myths surrounding the death penalty, Clay's enlightening and provocative analysis deals a staggering blow to the security blanket that capital punishment represents, and provides valuable ammunition to those who believe that the death penalty erodes respect for human life, breeds contempt for the legal system, and is, in the former words of former Supreme Court justice Arthur J. Goldberg, "the greatest conceivable degradation to the dignity of the human personality." Let us hope that the decade of the 1990s will see a return in American jurisprudence to a belief in the potential rehabilitation of criminals, to a reinsertion of the concept of mercy into sentencing, and to, as President Bush has stated, a "kinder, gentler vision of America."

—Dr. Jeffrey M. Elliot
Professor of Political Science
North Carolina Central University
Durham, North Carolina
May, 1989

PREFACE

A Few Words from Capitol Hill

This book reflects the personal opinions of a United States Congressman concerning the death penalty in America. It is not widely known, but should be, that the application of capital punishment in this country is largely reserved for those who are economically deprived and politically powerless. Only those who cannot afford first-class legal representation, including minorities, poor whites, and even the middle class, are victimized by this act of vengeance, which has been euphemistically called a "fitting retribution" for those who have callously disregarded the right of others to live.

Current popular support for capital punishment, and President Ronald Reagan's conservative appointments to the U.S. Supreme Court, have created a situation where the execution of thousands of convicted felons is only a matter of time. For approximately ten years, there were no executions in the United States. But since 1977, when Gary Gilmore was granted his wish to die in the state of Utah, more than 120 others have suffered the same fate. Over seventeen hundred convicts now sit on death rows in the thirty-seven states which still sanction the death penalty.

The writing of this book was prompted by Senator Strom Thurmond's 1981 introduction of a bill to re-establish the death penalty for some federal crimes. The Republican-controlled Senate approved the measure, but it was not passed by the House of Representatives. If it had been approved by both Houses of Congress, and signed by the President, acts of espionage, sabotage, treason, and murder on federal property would have become crimes punishable by death. The U.S. Senate argued that the new law would serve as a deterrent to those who might contemplate such crimes. But if such activities (despite recent news headlines) are relatively rare, as statistics indicate they are, then who is being deterred by such draconian measures?

In addition, this book explores some of the myths associated with various interpretations of the Bible as justifying capital punishment. Biblical verses are often used by unscrupulous men directly to contradict other Biblical passages of greater moral force. The absurdity of some scriptural texts, particularly in the Old Testament, challenges modern-day Christians to advance ethically and morally into the twenty-first century. I argue here that an "eye for an eye" was an attempt to place a limitation on violence, not an advocacy of more killing on behalf of the state.

Religious leaders of most of the major faiths are directly opposed to capital punishment, based on their own interpretations of Scripture. However, it is an unfortunate reality that a majority of those professing to follow the teachings of Christ ignore the beliefs of their own leaders and overwhelmingly support the death penalty. The danger of confrontation on the question of who has the ultimate moral authority in modern America is fully explored. I also examine the hypocrisy of many in the pro-life movement who decry the killing of the unborn while simultaneously embracing capital punishment for those already born.

Since this book is the result of information obtained from research in many different sources, it is impossible to give credit to each. But a special debt of gratitude is owed to those mentioned in the footnotes. Also, several individual friends, Germaine Grigsby and Jake Jasmine, deserve thanks for providing much information. In addition, Barbara McClure and Richard Rimbunas, analysts at the Congressional Research Service, The Library of Congress, researched much of the chapters on "The Death Penalty as a Deterrent" and "Discrimination and Capital Punishment." Bill Woldman of the Congressional Research Service, Library of Congress, provided all charts and graphs in Chapters IV and VI, and Mike and Mary Burgess edited the final manuscript. My many thanks to all who assisted in this endeavor.

—Rep. William L. Clay, Sr. (D-Mo.)
St. Louis, Missouri
July 4, 1989

I.

THE POSITION OF AMERICA'S RELIGIOUS LEADERS

Why is it necessary to kill people who kill people to teach people who kill people that killing people is wrong?

1. RELIGION AND CAPITAL PUNISHMENT

A common homily, neatly framed and found hanging ostentatiously on the walls of many Christian homes, serves as a constant reminder of our inability to deliberate the moral consequences of capital punishment with reason and common sense. This unimposing prayer from the Middle Ages states:

> God grant me the serenity to accept the things I cannot change, the courage to change the things I can, and the wisdom to know the difference.[1]

That sentence neatly sums up the moral imperative facing this nation in the continued use of capital punishment. Premeditated murders committed by individuals or by groups of individuals (incorrigible felons, vigilantes, *and* state governments) constitute wrongful acts under the most primitive set of ethical rules known to man. By confronting this issue openly, we can gain the wisdom to distinguish the moral dilemmas posed by capital punishment, and ultimately find the courage to take whatever steps are necessary to stop this morally repugnant practice once and for all.

The views of the American public concerning capital punishment reflect a basic paradox in religious values. Although a majority profess

15

belief in some version of Christianity, they fail to understand or embrace the fundamental philosophical tenets of most of the Christian churches to which they belong. Leaders from almost every Christian denomination or sect in the United States have firmly denounced capital punishment as contrary to the teachings of Jesus Christ. Church hierarchies argue that God's love is redemptive even for the most sinful of men. But the death penalty is irrevocable, and this precludes the possibility of reforming or restoring a human being to a normal or productive religious state.

The Reverend Guillermo Chavez, Chairman of the National Interreligious Task Force on Criminal Justice, has made the following observations:

> It is because our involvement in the religious community speaks to our being reconciled to God that we are challenged to counter the notion of retribution as epitomized in federally-sanctioned killing, with the sure knowledge of restoration as revealed in scripture.
>
> The state taking a human life precludes a reconciliation and restoration of that life to the society. But the religious community's understanding of the inherent power of restoration to reshape a self-willed murderer into a Moses, to deliver a raving bigot into a Paul the preacher, is not only a guidepost through its right action, but also the very ground of its existence. Therefore, the religious community as represented in the National Interreligious Task Force on Criminal Justice's membership, has a moral authority and the spiritual responsibility to lead the assault against state-sanctioned killings.[2]

At the very highest levels of almost all Christian authority this concept is considered basic to the teachings of the King of Kings, Jesus of Nazareth, who said: "I came that they may have life and may have it more abundantly."[3]

In establishing church dogma, the bishops, cardinals, prelates, priests, and presiding church officers have not been influenced or intimidated by the persistent advocacy of a majority of their flocks for capital punishment. Revenge, they say, may not be sought for its own sake. But an appreciable percentage of the Christian laity, instead of following the moral dictates of their leaders, have overwhelmingly agreed with those civil officials—presidents, governors, mayors, judges, and prosecutors—who have supported the death penalty as fitting retribution for criminal acts.

Despite the support of capital punishment by a majority of lay persons, two out of three American Church leaders strongly oppose it as an infringement on the dignity of life. Couching their opposition in biblical terms, they cite the admonition in the New Testament *Book of Romans*:

> To no man render evil for evil, but provide good things not only in the sight of God, but also in the sight of all men. If it be possible, as far as in you lies, be at peace with all men. Do not avenge yourselves, beloved, but give place to the wrath, for it is written, "Vengeance is mine: I will repay," says the Lord....Be not overcome by evil, but overcome evil with good.[4]

Each major religious denomination has gone on record, at national conferences, convocations, or synods, as being against the death penalty. Leaders of these gatherings argue that the ethics of Christianity are grounded largely in the New Testament, which begins with the birth of Christ and continues through his thirty-three years on earth until crucified at the hands of civil officials.

The New Testament themes of love, compassion, and forgiveness are the principle components of Western Christian beliefs. Passages from the Old Testament depicting God as furious, angry, and wrathful are explained as the inability of mortals to convey supernatural feelings. They are merely figures of speech to express God's displeasure with sin, and His determination to punish sinners.

Many verses of the Bible, including the Old Testament, bear out the conclusions of religious scholars that expressions of anger were only to be interpreted in the physical sense, not in the metaphysical.

Based upon these theological perspectives, ecclesiastical heads of most Christian faiths contend that state-imposed killing contravenes God's mission for man, just as Christ Himself supplanted and expanded upon the maxims and teachings of the Old Testament.

Yet, a majority of their followers dispute the right of church leadership to define the morality of this issue. Disagreements by such a large sector of the laity poses a serious threat to the highest echelons of church authority. The mere fact that most Christians demand the right in this instance to interpret morality for themselves is a contradiction of the faith they claim to profess. The consequences extend far beyond the question of capital punishment. Who has the right, the responsibility, the authority, even the obligation to decide questions of Christian morality? Can a person selectively choose, as a matter of individual conscience, which elements of church dogma he or she will or will not believe, and still claim to be a member of that body? Until such matters are resolved, the controversy and the challenges will continue unabated.

National polls show two out of three Christians (72%) in this country support capital punishment. Equally alarming are similar surveys stating that two out of three Americans also oppose protections afforded by the First Amendment to the Constitution; favor abolishing the Supreme Court; and support the re-establishment of corporal punishment in public schools. Finally, these same polls further reflect the sad truth that almost as many students now finishing high school may be functional illiterates, and that such percentages are even higher in the poorer neighborhoods of modern urban America. If nothing else, these surveys make a persuasive argument for going beyond popular referenda in arriving at nationally acceptable moral standards of conduct.

Rabbi Irwin M. Blank, Professor of Jewish Education at Baltimore Hebrew College, spoke rather pointedly to the question of popular referenda on moral issues when he said:

> The ultimate example of that is a section we read from the Torah just this past Sunday on Sodom and Gomorrah, and that is where you had an absolutely corrupt society, it was what the people wanted. But divine judgment reflected some other kind of attitude.[5]

2. THE CHURCHES SPEAK OUT AGAINST CAPITAL PUNISHMENT

Our society is experiencing an attack on human life—euthanasia, the idea of "death with dignity" (a euphemism), abortion, the violence and threat of life everywhere in the world. Capital punishment is another form of attack on the sanctity of human life....[6]

In their stringent opposition to the death penalty, church leaders have not contested the right of the state to exercise its functions of punishment, only to proscribe limits on its authority. They argue that forgiveness, compassion, and reconciliation must supersede our thirst for vengeance.

As stated by the General Conference Mennonite Church in its *Declaration on Capital Punishment*:

> God was in Christ reconciling the world to Himself.
> Today this ministry of reconciliation is entrusted to the
> disciples of Christ, God making His appeal through
> them...The state may use force, but not when it con-
> tributes to disorder more than order...In maintaining
> peace and order the state has a responsibility not only
> for the deterrence of crime and the restraint of the
> criminal....It has a responsibility as well for the rehabili-
> tation of the offender, enabling him to find a useful
> place in an orderly, peaceful society...The use of the
> death penalty, however, is a repudiation of the rehabili-
> tative aspect of the state's own task and function. In
> deliberately taking the life of the offender the state de-
> clares him beyond rehabilitation and removes him for-
> ever from the realm of the Church's redemptive min-
> istry. This, we believe, is an unjustified assumption of
> final judgment, a role which belongs to God alone."[7]

But "hell-and-brimstone" evangelists, monopolizing the Sunday morning airwaves on commercial television, often express views to the contrary. Their inflamed rhetoric, surpassed only by their equally profound ignorance of scripture, fills the tube with archaic Old Testament notions about the biblical mandate for "revenge." Reconciling these notions with Jesus's message of love and redemption seems almost impossible. Even though such religious pimps are revered by millions of physically-impaired shut-ins and an equal number of intellectually-deficient "shut-outs," they remain the exception in religious America—a fringe group whose peculiar ideas of Christianity can hardly provide a moral imperative on any vital questions of the day.

Official spokespersons for most organized Christian bodies in the United States emphatically state their consternation at the idea of capital punishment, labelling it "demeaning" to the value of human existence. They contend that capital punishment compounds the original capital crime, and further violates the moral order of society and the religious order of the community. Treating criminals as human trash to be burnt and discarded, they assert, demeans the humanity of all those involved in law enforcement, as well as those victims who have been violated by the crimes themselves. The issue has been lengthily and spiritedly debated at national religious conferences and seminars over the past two decades. At one such recent debate Bishop John Wesley Lord, of the Washington, D.C. Conference of the Methodist Church, stated:

> A Christian view of punishment must look beyond correction to redemption. It is our Christian faith that redemption by the grace of God is open to every repentant sinner, and that it is the duty of every Christian to bring to others by every available means the challenge and opportunity of a new and better life. We believe that under these circumstances only God has the right to terminate life.[8]

This affirmation of faith and dogma apparently leaves very little room for equivocation by Methodists on the subject of capital punishment, at least for those Methodists who believe in the right of Church hierarchy to decide questions of religious morality. There is no room here for individual interpretation. Bishop Lord speaks with the full authority of the Methodist Church when he challenges Christians to allow others an opportunity for a new and better life. Death precludes all such endeavors. The Methodist Church recognizes the value of individual life, and rightfully scorns the idea of human sacrifice, even of despised convicted felons.

In a similar statement of doctrine, the Episcopal Church adopted the following resolution at its 1958 General Convention:

> Inasmuch as the individual life is of infinite worth in the sight of the Almighty God; and whereas the taking of human life falls within the providence of the Almighty God and not within the right of man; be it resolved that the General Convention goes on record as opposed to capital punishment.[9]

Thus, Episcopalians have also been left with no flexibility for posturing on the question of their church's views concerning state-imposed murder. The General Convention of Episcopals (Clerical and Lay

officials) declared that only God has the power to take life.   Episcopalians who disagree with this stand are in clear defiance of their own
church's mandate.

The American Baptist Churches in the U.S.A. passed a similar
resolution in 1977, summarily rejecting capital punishment. It noted that
almost half of those on death row were from minority groups. Therefore,
the Baptist convention declared, capital punishment "...is immoral and
unjust."[10] This conclusion clearly pre-empts practicing Baptists, at the
very least, from claiming moral ambivalence on the discriminatory nature
of the death penalty. The fact that most Baptists oppose their leaders on
this question can be easily attributable to their traditional disregard for
centralized church authority.

The Christian Church (Disciples of Christ) went one step further
in a 1957 statement:

> Christian justification of punishment is always found in
> the hope of rehabilitation of the offender: since dead
> people cannot be rehabilitated we can in no way defend
> capital punishment on Christian grounds.[11]

This conclusion explicitly speaks to the concern of salvation, and
the opportunity for rehabilitation and restoration. Disciples of Christ
should have no problem in discerning the theological imperative of their
leaders on this question. Those who reject the position of their ministers
do so in a matter inconsistent with their own church dogma.

In 1966, the Lutheran Church in America adopted a stance similar to that of these other religious groups. Delegates to its national conference ratified the following statement:

> [The Conference] has urged abolition [of the death
> penalty] on the grounds that the penalty falls on the
> weakest groups in society, makes irrevocable any mis-
> carriage of justice, and ends the possibility of restoring
> the convicted persons to effective citizenship.[12]

That declaration of belief gives Lutherans ample ammunition to
support the traditional arguments against capital punishment. It must be
pointed out, however, that the Lutheran Church in America does not
speak for all Lutherans. Another faction of the church, the American
Lutheran Church, is much closer to the American Baptist Churches in the

USA in its fostering of the concept of independent churches. Unlike the Lutheran Church in America, which believes that its separate congregations derive authority from the Church as a whole, the American Lutheran Church leaves most decisions up to the local churches. To the best of my knowledge, it has neither condemned nor approved the idea of capital punishment.

The 197th General Assembly of the Presbyterian Church (U.S.A), meeting in June of 1985 in Indianapolis, reaffirmed its historical position opposing capital punishment. Seven hundred commissioners, consisting of voting delegates, clergy, and laymen, rejected the death penalty and urged its 3,100,000 church members to seek its abolition as a means of state punishment:

> Whereas, the use of the death penalty in a representative democracy places citizens in the role of executioner: Christians...cannot isolate themselves from corporate responsibility, including responsibility for every execution, as well as for every victim.[13]

The United Presbyterian Church, speaking through the voice of Reverend Guillermo Chavez, declared:

> The use of the death penalty tends to brutalize the society that condones it. In denying the humanity of those we put to death, even those guilty of the most terrible crimes, including espionage or treason, we deny our own humanity and life is further cheapened. Nothing is achieved by taking one more life or adding one more victim. By inflicting lethal punishment, society descends to the level of violence and cruelty which it rejects in criminal behavior. We must set an example based on values of compassion, decency, and reconciliation.[14]

Opposition to capital punishment by leaders of the Catholic Church is not just a passing concern. The Church aggressively speaks out, loudly and clearly, against the death penalty, but has had less success, it seems, in communicating its position to its own adherents.

The U.S. Catholic Conference (the perennial synod of the Catholic Bishops of America) declared in 1974 and again in 1980 its abhorrence of the death penalty. At the November 1980 meeting, the bishops issued a 3,500-word paper stating that their position on capital punishment was a "manifestation of our belief in the unique worth and dignity of each person, a creature made in the image and likeness of God."[15] The Catholic Church admits that society not only has a right but also a need to punish those who violate the law; but, while citing the need to protect the public from dangerous persons, they insist that such needs "neither require nor justify taking the life of the criminal, even in cases of murder."[16]

There can be no middle ground on this basic question of morality for practicing Catholics.

The Catholic Conference further stated:

> We believe that in the conditions of contemporary American Society, the legitimate purposes of punishment do not justify the imposition of the death penalty...In the first place, we note that infliction of the death penalty extinguishes possibilities for reform and rehabilitation...Second, the imposition of capital punishment involves the possibility of mistake...Third, the legal imposition of capital punishment in our society involves long unavoidable delays...Delay also diminishes the effectiveness of capital punishment as a deterrent...Fourth, we believe that the actual carrying out of the death penalty brings with it great and avoidable anquish for the criminal, for his family and loved ones, and for those who are called on to witness or to perform the execution...Fifth, in the present situation of dispute over the justifiability of the death penalty and at a time when executions have been rare, executions attract enormous publicity, much of it unhealthy, and stir considerable acrimony in public discussion...Sixth, there is a widespread belief that many convicted criminals are sentenced to death in an unfair and discriminatory manner...[17]

Edward D. Head, Bishop of Buffalo, who assisted in drafting the position paper for the Conference, further elaborated: "Our statement was grounded in the belief that the taking of life should not be answered by more violence in the taking of [more] life.[18]

The leadership of the American Catholic Church unalterably opposes capital punishment. Citing the same theological bases as members of other Christian denominations, the Church has concluded that capital punishment is an essentially immoral act. Its 1980 resolution passed the conference by a vote of 145 to 31, with 14 abstentions. Instead of resolving the issue, however, the Church's statements have caused serious division within the ranks of American Catholic laity.

Church leaders of all denominations subsequentially demonstrated unified opposition to capital punishment in a broad-based attack on Senate Bill 114, introduced in 1981 by Senator Strom Thurmond of South Carolina and Senator Dennis DeConcini of Arizona. It provided the death penalty for espionage, treason, assassination of the President, homicide on federal property, and homicide committed during the course of certain other federal crimes. A 1972 decision by the U.S. Supreme Court had prohibited capital punishment for federal crimes, even though it had been used only sparingly prior to the Court's pronouncement.

In a strongly worded letter, delivered to every member of the United States Senate, fourteen of the most prestigious religious leaders in America opposed the reinstatement of the death penalty via Senate Bill 114:

> The religious traditions which we represent share a common belief that all human life is sacred. We believe that every individual has a unique worth and dignity which is given by God....We believe that the penalty fails to achieve the goal of protecting society and in fact perpetuates this tragic cycle of vengeance and violence.[19]

The list of signatures on the letter reads like a "Who's Who" of American Judaeo-Christian notables: The Rt. Reverend John M. Allin, Presiding Bishop of The Episcopal Church (U.S.A.); Ross T. Bender, Moderator of the Mennonite Church General Assembly; Bishop James R. Crumley, Jr., The Lutheran Church in America; Arie R. Brouwer, General Secretary, Reformed Church in America; Rabbi Alexander M. Schindler, President of the Union of American Hebrew Congregations; Bishop H. Ellis Finger, Jr., President, Council of Bishops, The United Methodist Church; Avery D. Post, President, United Church of Christ; William P. Thompson, State Clerk of the General Assembly, United Presbyterian Church in the U.S.A.; Kenneth L. Teagarden, General Minister and President, Christian Church (Disciples of Christ); Stanley Bohn, Executive Secretary for Home Ministries, General Conference, Mennonite Church; James E. Andrews, State Clerk, the General Assembly of the Presbyterian Church; a representative from the General Board, Church of the Brethren; Rev. Monsignor Francis J. Lally, Secretary, Department of Social Development and World Peace, U.S. Catholic Conference; and Rev. Dr. Eugene Pickett, President, Unitarian Universalist Association of Churches in North America.

The fourteen signers of the petition opposing the Thurmond bill represent an awesome array of religious and moral power. They are all highly esteemed members of the clergy, recognized worldwide in their respective denominations. None of them could be even remotely considered liberal extremists, religious zealots, revolutionaries, or agitators attempting to cause grave damage to established theological tenets—or even to any secular Constitutional mandates. They are well-reasoned, responsible citizens who have arrived at their beliefs solely through their long and careful studies of the teachings of Jesus Christ. Christ's message is one of life, not death; his cry is consistently one of mercy, not revenge. If one truly professes to be a Christian—i.e., a follower of Christ—how can one possibly believe otherwise?

The introduction of the bill calling for restoration of the death penalty for certain federal crimes reflected the growing popular support for state-sponsored executions. The crimes for which it could be applied are virtually nonexistent—foreign spies are never executed these days, even in the Soviet Union, and domestic spies rarely commit crimes for which execution seems even remotely justifiable as punishment. Despite a total absence of evidence that these crimes are increasing to any significant degree, or that the imposition of the death penalty could have stopped those who have sold state secrets, the Senate in its collective wisdom passed the bill. The U.S. House of Representatives, however, did not concur.

On January 3, 1985, Representative George W. Gekas of Pennsylvania introduced H.R. 343, a bill to restore the death penalty for the federal crimes of homicide, treason, and espionage. Congressman Gekas issued a "dear colleague" letter to his 434 fellow members of the House, stating: "There is no need to engage in any more debate about the death penalty. We have seen the effects of a society without it: violent and senseless criminal acts and a dramatic and threatening increase in espionage-related activities."[20]

But even when the federal government *was* empowered to use the death penalty for civil offenses, it rarely imposed it. The only civilians ever convicted in a federal court for espionage and subsequently executed were Julius and Ethel Rosenberg, whose guilt or innocence is still a matter of much controversy. They, too, fit the criteria for exercising capital punishment in the United States: both were members of a minority group, the Jews.

3. THE REVOLT WITHIN THE CATHOLIC CHURCH

Recently, the Roman Catholic bishops of America suggested that the right-to-life movement expand its agenda to include poverty, hunger, nuclear war, and capital punishment. As a result, the split between leadership and laity has intensified, becoming a rancorous public debate between the churchmen in authority and ultra-conservatives within the ranks. If the bishops, who are pushing for the consolidation of these moral issues under one moral umbrella, are not more judicious in their ethical interpretations, they may soon find themselves the subject of petition drives demanding their recall.

Despite the guidance given by their religious leadership, most Christians seem incapable of establishing a logical link between "right to life" issues and the abolition of capital punishment. Religious leaders in turn seem baffled by their flocks' contradictory behavior.

Speaking to this point, the Catholic bishops of the United States have said:

> We do not wish to equate the situation of the criminals convicted of capital offenses with the condition of the innocent unborn or of the defenseless aged or infirm, but we do believe that the defense of life is strengthened by eliminating exercise of a judicial authorization to take human life.[21]

The American bishops are backed on this issue by the head of the Catholic Church, Pope John Paul II; a spokesman for the Vatican has stated:

> If we are going to be for life, we have to be for all life, not just in the womb...and this Pope is definitely for life.[22]

Pope Paul VI (who died in 1978) was perhaps the first pontiff to speak out against capital punishment. Although he did not declare executions immoral acts or forbid Catholics to support it, he stated that modern societies should have reached a level of civilization where capital punishment was not required. In his annual address to the Vatican diplomatic corps in January 1983, Pope John Paul II encouraged all heads of state and their governments to grant clemency or pardons to those sentenced to die. He said, "You can understand...why in its humanitarian concern, the Holy See is prompted to recommend clemency and grace for those condemned to death, especially those who have been condemned for political motives."[23]

In spite of this papal support, Joseph Cardinal Bernardin of Chicago, who first advanced the idea of merging other moral considerations with the "right-to-life movement," now finds himself under attack from right-wing Catholics. Robert M. Patrick of the Ad Hoc Committee in Defense of Life, Inc., has said:

> A broad range of pro-life leaders...are rejecting the Chicago Archibishop's demand that abortion be made just another issue among many others—ranging from poverty to a concern for human rights in El Salvador— because it would deny abortion's unique status as the nation's premier social issue.[24]

The organization's newsletter, *Lifeletter*, reported:

> The great majority of anti-abors [sic] reject linkage of abortion with anything else.[25]

In a similar reaction to Cardinal Bernardin's proposal, an anti-abortion group in Massachusetts adopted a resolution decrying "Any and every attempt to classify as pro-life any candidate...locally or nationally, who supports abortion, promotes abortion, or votes to fund abortion."[26] *The Catholic Eye*, the news organ of a conservative Catholic faction, has stated:

> Pro-abortion Catholic politicians like Senators Teddy Kennedy and Vermont's Pat Leahy can now claim to be as pro-life as, say, Henry Hyde or Jesse Helms—you know, they just take different sides.[27]

The Catholic bishops' statement makes it clear that it is inconsistent to cherish the life of the unborn, and at the same time demean the life of those already born. In the vernacular of the ghetto, the bishops are saying, "That bird won't fly," while their parishioners are saying, "A bird in the bush is more sacred than two in the hand."

One member of the pro-life movement, James Hitchcock, a professor of History at Saint Louis University, rejected Bishop Bernardin's wedding of abortion to capital punishment:

> The bishops want to shed the abortion albatross by changing the subject from abortion to the immorality of nuclear war.[28]

Others in the right-to-life movement are blunter. A board member of Missouri Citizens for Life said:

> Abortions and nuclear war are not analogous moral questions.[29]

It seems that the most ardent supporters of the pro-life movement have deliberately limited the issue in scope and time. Their actions lead one to believe, as Representative Barney Frank of Massachusetts has recently said, that (according to them), "life begins at conception and ends at birth." What transpires after the miracle of birth seems of far less consequence. Perhaps that explains why most pro-lifers oppose government funding of programs to clothe the naked, feed the hungry, and house the homeless, all ideas proposed by that greatest of revolutionaries, Jesus Christ. It also may explain how they rationalize their hawkish stances on war, on nuclear proliferation, and on toxic contamination of air and water. If life begins at conception and ends at birth, why should anyone give serious thought to what happens thereafter? Somehow, putting to death a thirteen-year-old boy in the electric chair at a state prison in Florida is seen as acceptable behavior by the same people who view the aborting of a thirteen-day-old fetus as sufficient reason for massive protest demonstrations. The National Right to Life Movement sponsors annual marches to Washington, D.C., to coincide with the anniversary of the 1973 Supreme Court decision (*Roe vs. Wade*) which held that the Constitution protects a woman's decision on whether or not to terminate her pregnancy. Although a new majority on the Supreme Court has been responsible for allowing states to begin taking the lives of some 1,700 prisoners now on death row, few (if any) of the protest signs in the annual pro-life marches from the White House to the Supreme Court have decried this particular assault on humanity.

The leadership of the pro-life movement undoubtedly has popular support among those rank-and-file Catholics who oppose their own bishops' position of equating this question with other moral issues. But once again this raises the basic question of who in the Church has the authority to interpret what is morally right; once again we see individuals deciding for themselves which tenets of faith they will accept, and which they will reject. If bishops and popes do not have the moral authority to decide such issues, who does?

The cavalier attitude of most pro-lifers concerning the morality of capital punishment must be conditioned on some mystical direct pipeline to an authority higher than that of Christ's representatives on Earth. In the Catholic Church the only living person with moral authority greater than the bishops is the pope, and he has consistently supported the Catholic bishops of America in their opposition to the death penalty. So, to whom do pro-lifers appeal their case—God Himself? So they would have us believe.

Mere mortals, those of us who do not enjoy the privilege of direct, two-way communication with the Creator, are not overawed at this prospect, but rather frightened and disillusioned. We are frightened that those who possess such a perverted sense of human value might be chosen as God's personal interpreters. We are disillusioned that such a mandate— the right to overrule accepted church leaders on issues of dogma—should be conferred on a group interested in just one moral question, however worthy in itself, while remaining wholly oblivious to the merits of other, equally important moral imperatives.

Since Cardinal Bernardin has linked other life-support issues with that of abortion, most leaders of the pro-life movement have been scrambling to capture the moral high ground. They continue to emphasize "abortion" as the only real ethical question on the modern political horizon. They have carefully avoided taking issue with the evils of nuclear war, the abandonment of the sick, the hungry, and the elderly, and have silently disregarded the evils of capital punishment. Each reveals his or her single-minded crusade for one issue by fanatically attempting to defeat all elected officials who disagree with them on the question of abortion. Enthusiastically embracing those officials who opposed the other so-called issues in the "right to life" struggle, exposes a chink in their ethical armor.

4. A FAULTY PUBLIC RELATIONS CAMPAIGN

The first and most important order of business at the 1984 Kansas City, Missouri convention of the Right to Life Committee was to endorse President Ronald Reagan for re-election. That position was based, according to all reports, solely on Mr. Reagan's stated opposition to abortion. Yet, every delegate in attendance was equally aware of Mr. Reagan's strong support of capital punishment, his avowed intention to decimate Aid to Dependent Children funds, his opposition to Medicare and Medicaid for the old and the impoverished, and his budget recommendations to cut or abolish food programs for the hungry.

Such actions must force the thinking public to view with suspicion the moral agenda of those in the pro-life movement. Their continuing effort to isolate or divorce the question of abortion from other life-supportive social issues has proven to be effective politically, but questionable morally.

The most ardent advocates of "right to life" issues have aligned themselves with intransigent elected officials who oppose programs for sustaining the lives of the underprivileged and/or non-whites. No matter how vociferously pro-lifers protest their stance as championing the rights of the poor, their true record speaks for itself.

The group's enthusiastic endorsement of President Reagan's re-election bid might have been considered an exception to this rule. But unswerving pro-life support for those members of Congress who consistently vote to cut or abolish programs sustaining the disadvantaged exposes the ultimate goal of the group. They are not remotely concerned with helping those already born and struggling to survive; or, in those few instances where such groups have expressed such concerns, they have tempered them with insistence that those receiving care rehabilitate themselves or submit themselves to religious lecturing. Most, however, have reduced their efforts to electing only those politicians who support their single-issue campaign, without taking into consideration whatever else that potential officeholder might endorse.

During the 99th Congress, 27 senators and 119 members of the House introduced or co-sponsored legislation to legalize the death penalty. Needless to say, most are viewed as heroes by the vast majority of those active in the pro-life movement. This lofty status is guaranteed merely by their simultaneous opposition to abortion.

The hypocrisy of those who mouth grave concerns for the starving children in rat-infested tenements, while silently condoning the sordid conditions under which they live, should be obvious even to casual observers. Supporting legislators who actively advocate war and destruction of human life in faraway places while denying needed aid to millions at home cannot be enshrined as "pro-life" in any sense.

The 99th Congress passed a bill appropriating $124 million for the development of binary chemical weapons. Twenty-two of the 27 pro-life senators voted for that measure; two others were absent. The most effective public relations campaign could not explain how such horrendous weapons, long outlawed by the Geneva Convention, could possibly be reconciled with basic values of human life. In the House, 103 supporters of pro-life issues cast votes to produce such weapons.

In like fashion, both chambers voted during this same session to appropriate $1.5 billion for 21 MX missiles, whose explosive capabilities represent the most destructive weapons ever conceived by man. Again, 24 of the 27 illustrious senators endorsed at the 1984 Right to Life Committee Convention voted to support this measure. In the House, 107 of the 119 followed suit. One must suppose that President Reagan's reference to MXs as "peace keepers" obviated any burden of guilt from the shoulders of those in the pro-life movement.

The position taken by pro-life organizations and their anti-abortion followers is a telling indictment of the shallow commitment many of them have to the sacredness of *all* life. Political expediency, not moral commitment, is the driving force behind efforts to champion the sacred right to life of the unborn. To suggest that Senator Jesse Helms, who opposes aid to dependent children, child nutrition programs, medical care for the aged, housing for the poor, and food stamps for the hungry, is somehow more *pro*-life than Senator Ted Kennedy, who spearheads the fight for these rights, seems almost sacrilegious. It demonstrates blind acceptance of a set of misguided priorities. Those espousing these views lack an all-encompassing vision of life, while possessing a massive insensitivity toward those parts of it which they find personally distasteful. Is this what Christ taught us?

There seems to be no middle ground, no possible room for compromise between pro-lifers and pro-choicers. The lines of contention are rigidly drawn. But there does seem to be a certain lack of unanimity among "right to lifers" themselves. The more inflexible ideologues take the position that all abortions, including those intended to save the life of a mother, are *per se* immoral and should be banned. The more radical elements within this group have casually resorted to terrorist acts reminiscent of the fanatical para-military anarchist groups of the 1960s. They have bombed abortion clinics, and threatened bodily harm to doctors who legally perform this legitimate medical procedure.

Others in this same movement are not as dogmatic in their positions. Some of them believe there is justification for aborting deformed or AIDS-diseased fetuses. Still others (including, apparently, George Bush) believe that rape, incest, or threats to the life of the mother constitute sufficient grounds for abortion.

My personal experiences with these groups have convinced me that their opinions vary widely, even within such organizations, often conflicting with each other. Many do not hesitate to support killings of other kinds—in self-defense, in war (justified or not), or via gas chambers or electric chairs. Their supposed position in favor of life impresses me (in most circumstances) as one determined more by circumstance or political considerations than by any moral dictate, and one very much subject to the winds of conservatism that blew through Washington in the 1980s. I am not saying that such persons are all insincere in their beliefs, only that the pro-life issue seems to have been fixed upon by many conservative groups as one means of gaining political support among fundamentalist Christians.

The more rabid pro-life groups seem incapable of considering other tragic examples of man's inhumanity to man. When President Nixon ordered the carpetbombing of Cambodia and North Vietnam during the closing days of the Vietnam War, killing thousands of innocent men, women, and children, no member of the pro-life movement spoke out. When the CIA plotted the murder of Salvador Allende, the democratically elected President of Chile (irrespective of his political philosophy), they remained silent. These were both measures favored by conservative politicians. Similarly, many "pro-lifers" were ecstatic when they learned of the senseless slaughter of non-combatant men, women, and children in Nicaragua and Panama, and loudly voiced their approval.

This is a simplification, of course; different individuals act for different reasons. Those working to recriminalize abortions represent a mixture of personalities encompassing all sides of the moral and political spectrum. Some are conservative, some liberal, some mere opportunists, and still others religious crusaders or profiteers. The only common thread unifying the movement is religious indoctrination: by and large, a disproportionate number of pro-lifers are members either of the Catholic Church or of various fundamentalist groups.

In spite of protestations that moral conviction, not religious belief, is the driving force behind their actions, evidence indicates otherwise. I too am a Catholic, born, bred, and educated, having graduated from Catholic grade and high schools, and from a Jesuit university. I was taught to respect the religious freedoms of others. What I learned from the Jesuits at Saint Louis University, in addition to being stimulated to seek truth through logical reasoning, was an appreciation for the First Amendment to the U.S. Constitution, and the importance of balancing tolerance of differing religious views with the protection of the rights of *all* believers.

It is all too easy to condemn those who think differently than we do. Every potential case of abortion must be given separate consideration, taking into account the woman's age, education, mental stability and capability, possible drug or alcohol addiction, economic ability, and her own choice in the matter. To me, it's a question of religious freedom, and the right under the U.S. Constitution to make a judgment affecting one's own body based on one's own theological or philosophical beliefs. Some religions do not regard abortion as the taking of a human life; some contend that body and soul do not join at the moment of conception, but only at birth. At any rate, I am not impressed by arguments of those pro-lifers who contend that no pregnancy under any circumstance should ever be terminated. I am also uncertain that a fetus should be considered a human being until it can at least sustain life on its own, in the third trimester. Should young women be encouraged willy-nilly to seek abortions? No, of course not, but neither should they be condemned outright if they feel driven to such a course. And I will not cast the first stone.

Pontificating on the preciousness of unborn life while villifying those who attempt to alleviate the sufferings of those already born is myopic and unrealistic. The Catholic Bishops of America may not be victorious in their struggle to expand the agenda of the anti-abortion movement, but they are divinely justified in their efforts to equate other life-saving issues with that of abortion.

5. THE BIBLICAL CONFLICT

What we usually pray to God is not that His will be done, but that He approve of ours.[30]

State-imposed death is not a generic appendage analogous to any theological premise, but the result of real-life political decisions and determinations. Inevitably, there are those who will recite religious justifications to support the state's immoral actions. But upholding the right of the government to execute its citizens cannot be accomplished by lifting, out of context, specific verses from the Bible. Executions, in order to be legal, must be buttressed by an affirmative act of state legislators. The government, not the Bible, creates the situation whereby one human being pulls the switch or drops a cyanide capsule to terminate the life of another.

A single passage from the Old Testament of the Bible provides for many people sufficient moral validity for supporting capital punishment. From the phrase, "an eye for an eye," they erect a theological basis from which they seek to rationalize government-inflicted homicide. Nothing short of revenge drives those who use this passage as an underpinning for the justification of capital punishment. Convenient quotations and tasteful utterances do not alter reality. The hypocrisy of such mental gyrations in the defense of state-approved murder was reduced to its irreversible common denominator by philosopher Albert Camus, who wrote:

> Let us call it by the name which, for lack of any other nobility, will at least give the nobility of truth, and let us recognize it for what it is essentially: revenge.[31]

The full text of the "eye for an eye" passage actually paints with a wide brush numerous human acts abhorrent to civilized people. Other sections of that parable are so outlandish, so unreasonable, so contrary to any just code of ethics, that we can readily perceive why they are not quoted in defense of the death penalty. For example, part of the passage specifies exactly when an eye will literally be plucked, and that

> a kidnapper, whether he sells his victim or still has him when caught, shall be put to death...whoever curses his father or mother shall be put to death...when a man strikes his male or female slave with a rod so hard that the slave dies under his hand, he shall be punished. If, however, the slave survives for a day or two, he is not to be punished, since the slave is his own property.[32]

The next section is even more preposterous. Chapter 21 of *Exodus*, verses 22, 23, and 24, states:

> When men have a fight and hurt a pregnant woman, so that she suffers a miscarriage, but not further injury, the guilty one shall be fined as much as the woman's husband demands of him, and he shall pay in the presence of the judges. But if injury ensues, you shall give

life for life, eye for eye, tooth for tooth, hand for hand...."[33]

These words from the code of a primitive Middle Eastern society sanction human slavery, cater to the notion that women are the exclusive property of men, and advocate vengeance as a means of resolving all human differences. How ironic that supposedly intelligent people of seemingly genuine religious persuasion can use such intolerance to justify the moral efficacy of capital punishment.

Does the Bible thus command twentieth-century society to kill a child who is the victim of physical and/or sexual abuse by a parent, merely because he curses his mother or father? Does it suggest contempt for the rights of women? According to this verse, a man striking a pregnant woman shall be punishable only to the extent of the injury inflicted, and then only for damages demanded by her husband. What authority gives a man the sole right to make that determination? The woman's rights, her health, her safety, her feelings, all are reduced to secondary importance here. According to the Old Testament, women exist exclusively in the perceptions of men. More significantly, perhaps, one can infer from this passage that the Bible, through divine revelation, condones and embraces the barbarism of human slavery.

During the eighteenth and nineteenth centuries, American Christians who rigorously taught adherence to the "eye for eye" system of justice were not morally outraged when other Christians kidnapped tens of thousands of Black Africans and sold them into slavery to other Christians. Economics, not ethics, obviously influenced the latters' religious interpretation of this Bible passage. Mistreatment of slaves (according to the Old Testament) is not prohibited, and is, in fact, quite appropriate if properly applied. Only a master who beat his slaves so severely that they immediately died was to be punished. Jokingly, it can be argued that a master skillful in using the lash might even be canonized if the slave lived for two weeks, three days, two hours, ten minutes. Or it could mean any number of other things. But what it does say quite unequivocally is that one man has the God-given right to own another man, and also the option to physically abuse that human being.

One need not look far to see that strict application of the above quoted passages is contradicted in the Bible itself. According to scripture, all kidnappers, regardless of the severity of the offense, must be executed. This passage offers an excellent example for not relying wholly on the Bible for support of current philosophical and moral attitudes, particularly in the Old Testament.

This tenet lies in stark contrast to the story in the Book of *Genesis*, the first book of the Old Testament, which tells of the selling of Joseph by his brothers. Two of them plot to kill him and put his body in a cistern, claiming that a wild beast had devoured him. A third brother, Reuben, persuades them merely to leave him for dead. Should Reuben have also been killed for his complicity in the crime? Even more contradictorily, when the scheme finally unfolds Joseph says to them:

> Do not fear; can I take the place of God?...You intended evil against me, but God intended it for good, to do as he has done today, namely, to save the lives of many people. Therefore do not fear, I will provide for you and your dependents.[34]

Another obvious contradiction to these passages is the Sixth Commandment. When Moses descended from Mount Sinai carrying two stone tablets with the ten commandments inscribed, among them was a line that clearly proclaimed, "Thou shalt not kill." Here again we see the difficulty of using one passage to justify an entire theological system. Moses, incensed that Aaron had encouraged the building of a golden calf for the people to idolize, immediately sinned against the Sixth Commandment by ordering the Levites to *kill* three thousand of their own kinsmen. By issuing that order, Moses demonstrated yet another problem with using the Bible to defend capital punishment. There are too many incidents in the Holy Book which are grossly inconsistent. The Sixth Commandment does not mention any exceptions to the rule. It specifically does not say that Moses may order the deaths of thousands of people. It also does not state that individuals other than Moses can kill, or that the state (which is composed of individuals) has the right to execute criminals. Nor does it say that killing for vengeance is proper, while that for greed is not. It merely says, "Thou shalt not kill." It gives no special license, written or unwritten, to any agent of God or emissary of the state. And there are no special powers reserved for the social barons to stray or ignore the dictates of this commandment.

6. THE FIRST CAPITAL OFFENSE

What is one to think of the first capital offense? How can its biblical passage be reconciled with those used as a defense for capital punishment? Scripture records the first man-child born to Adam and Eve as Cain, a tiller of the fields; the second, his brother Abel, a keeper of the flock. It is written that Cain brought to the Lord an offering of the fruits of the soil, but that it was rejected. Infuriated that Abel's gift of the firstlings of his flock was pleasing to the Lord, Cain lured Abel into the fields and slew him in cold blood. That incident, motivated by the distorted emotions of hate and envy, became the first first-degree premeditated murder, the first capital offense documented in history. When the Lord said to Cain, "Where is your brother Abel?," he answered, "I do not know. Am I my brother's keeper?"[35]

Despite his anger and outrage, the Lord, the ultimate prosecutor, the most just of all judges, the only creator of life, did not condemn Cain to death. Even though the blood of Abel cried out for vengeance, the Lord Almighty did not strike Cain dead. Instead, in a decree more consistent with the New Testament and more attuned to the teachings of Jesus Christ, Cain was banished (segregated from society) to dwell in the Land of Nod, East of Eden, for the remainder of his life. Scripture tells us that the Lord retaliated with restraint. The Lord said, "When you till the soil, it shall not give its fruit to you; a fugitive and a wanderer shall you be on the Earth." Cain said to the Lord,

> "My punishment is too great to bear. You are driving me today from the soil; and from your face I shall be hidden. And I shall be a fugitive and wanderer on the Earth, and whoever finds me will kill me." But the Lord said to him, "Not so! Whoever kills Cain shall be punished sevenfold."[36]

What more evidence is needed to dispel the erroneous conclusions drawn by strict biblical constructionists who support capital punishment? Surely, before they examined the gory passages in the Books of *Exodus*, *Leviticus*, and *Numbers*, they read about the first murder committed by and against a human being in the Book of *Genesis*. How can they not observe the charity and compassion meted by God? What validity do they place on interpretation of an "eye for an eye" that cannot be repudiated by Cain's more just punishment?

Even more importantly, Christianity itself is an outgrowth of the direct repudiation or reinterpretation of most of the passages in the Old Testament. The position of Christians who advocate capital punishment is in direct contradiction to the founder of Christianity, Jesus Christ, and his

Sermon on the Mount. They are summarily dismissing his teachings, especially the admonitions embodied in that sermon. Jesus said:

> You have heard that it was said, "An eye for an eye,"
> and, "A tooth for a tooth." But I say to you not to re-
> sist the evildoer; on the contrary, if someone strike thee
> on the right cheek, turn to him the other also; and if
> anyone would go to law with thee and take thy tunic,
> let him take thy cloak as well; and whoever forces thee
> to go for one mile, go with him two.[37]

Theologians have themselves contended for centuries that the "eye for eye" verse in the Old Testament, instead of promoting more violence, was attempting to place restraints on the bloody feuds common among the primitive tribes of Israel. When put in historical perspective, this view seems a reasonable assessment. During that period of time, retaliation amongst the various Israeli sects was so extensive that wise men thought it better to impose a system allowing for "only" an eye for an eye, "only" a life for a life, "only" a tooth for a tooth. Prior to that time it was common practice to slaughter entire families to retaliate for the killing of a single kinsman. Such feuds continued for generations, as they do today in the Middle East, one violent abuse prompting another. Holy Scripture says in *Proverbs* 25:2, "God has glory in what he conceals, kings have glory in what they fathom."[38]

Religious fundamentalists in the United States liberally interpret the Bible as sanctioning the death penalty. Repeated references to texts from the Old Testament to justify its usage have become the hallmark of every tent-pitching and television-preaching evangelist.

Ignorance, the sin of which they are guilty, is equally as dangerous to civilization as the crimes of murder and rape. Interpreting biblical codes of morality three thousand years old without examining later standards set forth in the Talmud for establishing the proper punishments for exceeding the parameters of acceptable conduct, is nothing short of demagoguery. Rabbinic law was a safeguard to permissive use of capital punishment. Only on rare occasions was it allowed, and even then only under the most unique circumstances.

If Christians of today want to use biblical passages as the basis of their support for capital punishment, then they must study the circumstances under which they were written, trace the changing philosophical positions of those who first advocated them, and review the current need for their continued use. Such an endeavor would prove quite revealing to those really seeking something other than confirmation of predetermined beliefs.

They will find that nearly two thousand years ago, the Mishnah and Gemara, authoritative bodies of Jewish tradition, virtually eliminated taking the lives of those found guilty of criminal acts. Talmudic scholars since then have dismissed ancient Hebrew law as a basis for supporting capital punishment. Even under Jewish law it was almost impossible to reach a judgment in support of capital punishment. Circumstantial evidence was not permissible in testimony before the Sanhedrin (twenty-three judges sitting *en banc*). Nothing less than two eyewitnesses to the crime had to testify in person. And a more restrictive provision of the Mishnah (one of two books comprising the Talmud) required that the accused must have been advised in advance of his action that the crime was punishable by death.

It's no great mystery why executions in ancient Jewish society were rarities. The Talmud holds that "A Sanhedrin which executes a criminal once in seven years is called a 'court of destroyers'."[39] So, if the Jews put the law to the tests of time, relevancy, and justice, carefully scrutinizing its validity, and subsequently abandoned it as excessive, Christians today are surely obligated to at least study the issue.

Capital punishment, although technically legal, is not practiced in the state of Israel today, not even in the most fanatical cases of terrorism. Israeli law does prescribe the maximum penalty of death by hanging, but it is not mandatory, and has only been used once in that nation's thirty-seven-year history. The one exception to this rule was the execution of Adolf Eichmann, who was hanged May 31, 1962 in Jerusalem for crimes against humanity perpetrated during the Second World War. The decision to take his life, though popularly supported within the country, was by no means unanimous. It is still the subject of much controversy among those who value social order in that nation. Despite the fact that Eichmann was executed for crimes committed before the state of Israel came into existence, the debate among pro- and anti-capital punishment foes continues to rage.

The Israeli government was recently confronted with an equally perplexing moral problem, the trial of a Ukrainian immigrant, John Demjanjuk, extradited by the U.S. for the alleged murder of thousands of Jewish civilians at the Treblinka death camp during World War II. He denied ever having been at the camp, and asserted that he was also a prisoner and victim of Nazi torture during the war.

Once again, the state of Israel was forced to grapple with a life-

and-death decision involving the very moral fabric of their religious beliefs. Israeli courts had first to decide if Demjanjuk was innocent or guilty, and then if he deserved life in prison or death at the hands of a revengeful people. They chose to sentence him to death (in April of 1988) for crimes against humanity. His case is still being appealed, and the sentence, if affirmed, may never be carried out. Who can argue convincingly that Nazi war criminal Joachim von Ribbentrop suffered more by execution after the Nürnberg Trials than Rudolph Hess, who spent his last forty-two years in solitary confinement, before finally taking his own life?

The debate rages on among Christians because of weaknesses in the biblical arguments of those supporting state-sanctioned killing. Despite the impressive credentials of some of these enthusiasts and their apparent sincerity, too often they fail the test of sound reasoning and intellectual clarity when interpreting biblical positions. Their erroneous conclusions emerge as personal preferences based solely on blind faith. Their positions depend more on specific times and circumstances than on any tangible moral principles. The simplistic reading of the ambiguous "eye for an eye" text is rejected outright by most knowledgeable students of theology.

Critics and even some allies of those predicating their case for capital punishment solely on Holy Scripture share serious doubts about the logic of such arguments. They contend that substantial evidence exists to refute their credibility. Those who elevate the significance of the "eye for an eye" language to an infallible status fail in their mission precisely because they either have not read with comprehension the entire verse, or have deliberately chosen to ignore its import. Narrow interpretations serve only to discolor the issue. None of these arguments are convincing or worthy of belief. Neither the vengeful tone of the "eye for an eye" passage nor the gentle but unrealistic philosophy of the Sermon on the Mount establish an ideal set of rules for determining all human behavior. Strictly constructionist interpretations of either are formulae for disaster in a rapidly changing and developing world.

On the one hand, turning the "other cheek" suggests to many a somewhat soft stance on criminal activities; at the same time, reasonable, fair-minded individuals can certainly address the harsh realities of a crime-ridden society without resorting to the ultimate penalty.

I detest crime as much as anyone—I live and work in a city where the murder rate continues to reach new heights with each passing year—and I support any reasonable effort to rid our streets of neurotic, pathological killers. I understand the physical, mental, and psychological suffering of crime victims, and I empathize with the emotional strains imposed on them and their relatives by unreasonable and unreasoning violence.

Fortunately, those of us who disagree with the majority on this issue have not yet been branded as subversives and shipped out to labor camps, as in Nazi Germany, although there are right-wing groups whose programs, if fully carried out, would point in this direction. I believe that not only do we have the right to disagree with those who support state-sponsored murder, but the obligation to educate those who have not taken the time to familiarize themselves with this aberration of American criminal justice.

Capital punishment is *not* the only possible response to our increasing crime rate. It is, in fact, probably the *least* effective action we can take, and certainly the *most* damaging to our way of life. It is divisive by its very nature, as we have already seen, consuming enormous amounts of time, effort, money, and other resources, while exacerbating the violent behavior patterns of ordinary citizens, and thus creating an atmosphere conducive to increasing crime levels and vigilanteism.

The most I can say for capital punishment is that it's a convenient way for "macho" men to publicly display their disgust while concealing their helplessness. It serves to massage their egos and at the same time reassures them that John Wayne is alive and kicking. No societal good is discernible.

I believe that incorrigible criminals, serial murderers, and pathological killers should be dealt with in a manner appropriate to their crimes. They should neither be pampered nor excused, not for their social status, not for their economic backgrounds, not for any other reason. They must be held accountable for their actions. But I also believe that a society which creates conditions conducive to the development of violent crime and criminals must bear some of the responsibility for the result. We do not operate in a societal vacuum. Therefore, an attempt must be made to distribute ultimate responsibility equally among the guilty parties.

If all of those convicted of murder and sentenced to death are racial minorities and poor whites, then race and poverty are clearly compelling stimuli for committing murder. Otherwise, non-blacks of financial means would commit murder to the same degree. If wealthy whites and non-whites do commit murder and are rarely (if ever) executed, then other factors must come to bear. And if those mitigating factors include social position, an ability to influence prosecutors, or the means to hire the most qualified legal counsel, then I must reason that race and economic status *do* play a major role in our supposedly Christian society's dispensing of its most dastardly form of "justice."

This is what puzzles me about supporters of capital punishment who base their beliefs on biblical quotations: If society followed to the letter the demonic recommendations of an "eye for an eye," life in the United States would become harsh, cruel, ultimately unlivable. If pursued to the "nth" degree, the exhortation of the Sermon on the Mount might seem naive in its approach to human realities; yet it is still a more Christian formula for living than the "eye for an eye" philosophy. Both must be viewed as a set of values deriving from a specific time and culture, attempts to circumscribe behavior which had exceeded acceptable societal norms. The former emphasized the animalistic nature of man and established a code of action satisfying his thirst for revenge, while the latter appealed to man's spiritual inclinations and urged a more tolerant, more merciful response by those hurt and humiliated.

Somewhere between draconianism and sentimentalism lies the basis for a fairer code of ethics than the one presently permeating the courts of the United States of America.

Man knows instinctively the difference between right and wrong. But while that does not stop him from trampling on the rights of others, it does often make him defensive in protecting his own turf. Perhaps this explains how proponents of the death penalty flit about society with nary a tinge of guilt or conscience. Their right to life is so precious that anyone who threatens it has *no* right to life. This is, of course, an exaggeration and oversimplification of the self-preservation school of thought, but it seems appropriately applied in this case.

II.

ROMAN JUSTICE

It is the deed that teaches, not the name we give it. Murder and capital punishment are not opposites that cancel one another out but similars that breed their kind.

—George Bernard Shaw

1. THE LEGACY OF THE ROMAN EMPIRE

The Roman Empire left several important legacies to the world at large. Accomplishments of the Romans in agriculture, trade, transportation, education, art, and law are the foundations for many modern-day governments. The United States and Western Europe, in particular, are indebted to them for their legal systems. The Romans provided for us at least three legal pillars upon which we developed our system of jurisprudence: (a) the concept of equity, which states that circumstances often alter different cases and that the punishment should be flexible enough to fit specific crimes; (b) the idea that all laws must come from a single source, with power vested in a central body; and (c) the principle that all persons have characteristics in common which require universality and fairness in applying the law.

The application of the death penalty in the United States violates all three of these rules. Firstly, the failure of our legal system to consider race and poverty as potentially extenuating circumstances in capital crimes tramples the concept of judicial equity. Secondly, the fact that thirty-seven states use capital punishment while thirteen others do not, contravenes the concept of a central body of laws uniformly and fairly applied nationwide. Thirdly, the execution of poor and minority members of the population far out of proportion to their numbers must *per se* remove all pretense of justice in the application of this most final of punishments, and again dispel any notion of the universal application of the law.

Many of our citizens fail to understand just how indiscriminately the death penalty was applied against Christians in earlier centuries. In Roman times, Christianity was considered not merely sacrilegious, but a criminal subversion of the state-sponsored religion. And if today the primary factors leading to actual executions by the state are murder + race + poverty, tomorrow might see a broader application of the death penalty to political or religious crimes, either here or abroad. I do not claim that such an event is likely in the United States, but the strains of intolerance have always lain just below the surface in this country, and could surface under the pressures of severe social or economic turbulence.

So many so-called Christians fail to see any connection between past and present; perhaps it is just the "American way" to ignore the lessons of history. There are actually very few recognizable differences between the death sentences imposed on criminals in the United States today, and those forced on the Christians who faced the lions in the Roman Colosseum. The fact that, in the eyes of the Roman government, the Christians posed a security threat to the public safety, is not and never was a justifiable reason to legally sanction or morally sanctify the act of governmental homicide. If it had been, then the Romans would have been perfectly within their rights to execute these subversives for threatening the stability of the state.

Roman law did differ from American law in at least one respect, since it provided the means for the rehabilitation of the accused. Those convicted of defying the official state religion could redeem themselves and escape their death sentences by renouncing their beliefs in the teachings of Christ. Ironically, in today's "civilized" society, supposedly far advanced from the Roman era, criminals can find no such redemption, no possiblity of mercy or rehabilitation. Most American death sentences are final, albeit often long-delayed, since the vast majority of our politicans fear the potential political repercussions of commuting death sentences to life in prison without the possibility of parole. Like Gov. Pontius Pilate before them, they will let the legal system grind mercilessly forward to its ultimate conclusion, while washing their hands of the entire affair. "It's the will of the people," they say. "Poppycock!" I say.

And if today's Christians are, by and large, law-abiding, God-fearing individuals, so too were most citizens of ancient Rome. Modern-day Americans overwhelmingly believe that accusation by a prosecutor, indictment by a grand jury, a public trial, conviction, and sentencing to death by a judge, satisfies the weighty criteria of the due process of law.

Once the full panoply of a criminal's legal rights has been exhausted, more or less (too often less), the repulsive means become the standard for justifying the equally ugly end. No serious thought is ever given to what we are doing to ourselves as a society—or why; and how we have usurped the power and right of the Almighty to give or take life. Now we mask our actions with the trappings of law, hiding them within the panoply of judicial actions, legal motions, and pronouncements from the bench. In Roman times things were simpler—and less hidden. The emperors believed themselves infallible, and certainly had the political will (and the power) to remove their enemies and to shape the course of political events as they wished; the arbitrariness of their actions was evident for all to see. We prefer to clothe our actions with a sheen of self-righteousness, but the exercise of the ultimate punishment is in many ways just as arbitrary today as it was two thousand years ago.

Christians often see no contradiction to the laws of God or nature in taking the life of another human being, so long as it is sanctioned by the state through the majesty of the court. Neither did the vast majority of Roman citizens. Most Americans support legal executions, despite the obvious imperfections of a process which has led to the execution of innocent persons, not just in Roman times, but in the 1980s and '90s. Romans also saw no contradiction in feeding self-avowed Christians to the lions, or in crucifying political dissidents; by their tenets, these were necessary actions to maintain the public order. What we now see as barbaric, cruel, and unusual punishments they regarded as just and fitting retribution.

Thousands of Christians were herded into amphitheaters and executed in a grotesque form of live theatre. The Colosseum at Rome, most famous of the amphitheaters, was the scene of countless slaughters carried out in the name of law and order. The Circus Maximus, built by Tarquinius Priscus to seat 150,000 spectators (more than any sports stadium in the U.S.), witnessed dreadful human sacrifices under the rule of Domitian, Trajan, Septimius Severus, Decius, Valerian, and Diocletian. The victims' only offense, in most cases, was the practice of an illegal, subversive worship called Christianity.

Once the Romans had established the legality and morality of the death penalty, nothing could confine its application to such trivia as believing in a different god. Why then should equally imperfect Americans limit the imposition of their death penalty to such sordid crimes as murder, rape, and treason? There were no such limitations in earlier civilizations. Death was the prescribed penalty in antiquity for adultery, fornication, and sodomy; in some cultures it was even applied to female newborns, the sick, the aged, and the physically handicapped. Other societies employed it for such petty crimes as pickpocketing, stealing, and purse-snatching. Ironically, Sir Thomas More, Lord Chancellor of England, was beheaded for refusing to accept Henry VIII as head of the English Church.

In my own lifetime we have seen state-sponsored slaughter on an unprecented scale, culminating in the massacre of six million Jews by Adolf Hitler and the wholesale murder of ten or twenty million Ukrainian peasants and political enemies by Josef Stalin in the 1930s and '40s. Both Hitler and Stalin were born into Christian families and attended Christian schools; Stalin even briefly studied at an Orthodox seminary. Their experiences serve to dramatize only too well what can happen when individuals assume, under the banner of law, that they have the absolute right to murder others under a judicial umbrella.

Even in America the original thirteen colonies, from their birth until some time after the American Revolutionary War, had laws requiring the death penalty for such offenses as idolatry, adultery, blasphemy, striking one's mother or father, denying the existence of a true God, witchcraft, and sodomy. In some colonies, persons were subject to execution for trading with Indians, killing horses (or chickens or dogs) without permission, burglary, or even stealing grapes.

By the time of the War for Independence, the public had become disillusioned with government, and many jurors and judges were refusing to convict those accused of crimes where death was mandatory.

But that compassionate attitude did not extend past the boundaries of the thirteen colonies. Westward expansion of the country saw a revival of the "cheap life" mentality. Early settlers on the frontier were hanged for cattle-rustling, herding sheep in cattle country, having sex wth sheep, stage-coach robbery, and horse-stealing. Before, during, and after slavery, Blacks were executed for whistling at white women, reckless "eye balling," petty theft, or just being in the wrong place at the wrong time. But by no means has the controversy over capital punishment been confined to the New World or our young nation.

2. CAPITAL PUNISHMENT PREDATES THE BIRTH OF CHRIST

The debate surrounding the death penalty is as old as recorded history, predating the New Testament by centuries. Societies more culturally advanced than ours grappled with the consequences, the legality, the morality, and the practicality of capital punishment thousands of years ago. Ancient scholars, thinkers, and theologians, much less susceptible to the kinds of mundane pressures exerted by twentieth-century religious ideologues, raised serious questions about state-imposed capital punishment. Witness the statement of Diodotos, the son of Eucrates, in his address to the Athenian Assembly in 427 B.C., opposing a decree condemning the Mytilenaeans to death:

> To many offenses less than theirs states have affixed the punishment of death; nevertheless, excited by hope, men still risk their lives. No one when venturing on a perilous enterprise ever yet passed a sentence of failure on himself...all are by nature prone to err both in public and private life, and no law will prevent them.
>
> Men have gone through the whole catalogue of penalties in the hope that, by increasing their severity, they may suffer less at the hands of evildoers...as time went on and mankind continued to transgress, they seldom stopped short of death. And still there are transgressors. Some greater terror then has yet to be discovered; certainly death deters nobody. For poverty inspires necessity with daring; and wealth engenders avarice in pride and insolence; and the various conditions of human life, as they severely fall under the sway of some mighty and fatal power through the agency of the passions lure men to destruction.
>
> Desire and hope are never wanting, the one leading, the other following, the one divising the enterprise, the other suggesting that fortune will be kind; and they do immense harm, for, being unseen they far outweigh the dangers that are seen. Fortune too assists the illusion, for she often presents herself unexpectedly and induces states as well as individuals to run into peril, however inadequate their means; and states even more than individuals, because they are throwing for high stake, freedom or empire, and because when a man has a whole people acting with him, he exaggerates the importance of his aims out of all reason.
>
> In a word then, it is impossible, and simply absurd to suppose, that human nature when bent upon some favorable project can be restrained by the power of law or by any other terror.[1]

This controversy has continued for generations. The majority of societies that we have called "advanced" eventually abolished capital punishment. The reasons cited were various and sundry; ultimately, however, they all concluded that capital punishment is anathema to a civilized people.

The debate surrounding capital punishment has produced a large body of writing, but little real justification for its use. After thoroughly measuring its effects, most nations in the western world stopped executing criminals in the first half of the twentieth century. Most democratic governments in Western Europe, with the exception of Liechtenstein and Belgium, have either abolished by law or by custom the imposition of capital punishment; and the latter countries have not actually imposed the death penalty within living memory. Those states which have abolished capital punishment by law include Austria, Denmark, Finland, France, the Federal Republic of Germany, the Holy See, Iceland, Luxembourg, Monaco, the Netherlands, Norway, Portugal, and Sweden. We can expect the states of Eastern Europe shortly to follow suit, now that they have been freed from the Soviet yoke.

Nations which have abolished the death penalty for all crimes except those committed in exceptional circumstances (such as wartime), include Canada, Malta, San Marino, Spain, Switzerland, and the United Kingdom. Israel falls into the group which has abolished capital punishment except for crimes of genocide. Even Japan, our fierce opponent in World War II, excoriated for the brutality of its occupation forces, has only executed five persons in the past thirteen years. In Australia the individual states are divided on the issue in much the same way as in the United States.

The United States is the only major nation in the free world that still arbitrarily and capriciously engages in capital punishment on any large scale. We share the company of such repressive dictatorships as Albania, Cuba, North Korea, The People's Republic of China, Vietnam, and many Third World countries in Africa and the Middle East. Our Latino neighbors in Central and South America, whom so many Americans regard with prejudiced eyes, have largely abolished the death penalty except for drug-related crimes.

During the late 1970s, Pakistan executed 800 persons. South Africa, one of the most repressive police states in the world, executed 132 persons in 1978 (all except one was Black). Do we really wish to be associated with such regimes?

3. EXECUTIONS THROUGHOUT HISTORY

In order to assess how far we have advanced, a further comparison between today's standards and those of earlier times is instructive. There is remarkably little difference between the ways in which our nineteenth-century Western frontiersmen, the early Romans, and present-day Americans have defined the types of crimes punishable by death, and the ways in which "humane" methods for disposing of the guilty have been developed. The act of execution and the public's abnormal fascination for the process of determining who shall be executed has not changed much from age to age. One major (possibly beneficial) difference is that both Roman and frontier courts provided (at least in theory) swift, uniform decisions for all violaters of the law. Our present system is neither swift nor uniform, nor does it demand that all who commit heinous crimes be executed.

Approximately twenty thousand homicides are committed annually in this country; the number increases each year. Approximately four thousand persons are actually convicted of first-degree murders during the same period. Of these, perhaps two hundred may actually be sentenced to death, and twenty to fifty actually executed, often after long delays. The length of time from conviction, through a number of state and federal appellate courts, review by the U.S. Supreme Court, remanding back to lower courts, can take as long as ten years.

During 1985, eighteen executions were carried out in seven different states. All took place in the South. The average length of time between sentencing and execution was five years and eleven months.

Aimless days and sleepless nights, frigidly waiting in a cell block, never knowing, never really wanting to know when news of an appeal is denied, drives many on death row into a state of insanity. Philip Brasfield, who actually experienced such an ordeal, describes it in this way:

> Once sentenced to death, one begins endless months of waiting for the trial transcript to be typed and certified by the District Court before the process of an appellate brief can even begin. More months pass until the attorneys can prepare the defendant's arguments and submit them to the Court of Criminal Appeals. Then even more time is spent while the state answers the defendant's brief. Finally, the oral arguments are presented to the court, and the waiting con-

tinues until the court can reach a decision which will either reverse the sentence, resulting in a new trial or a commuted sentence, or affirm the sentence. The latter usually results in federal appeals and petitions to the Supreme Court. In short, a man convicted of a capital offense can expect to be caged, waiting for and thinking about his death, for as short as two years and as long as ten or fifteen or more. In fact, Caryl Chessman waited for twelve years on California's death row before losing his bid for life imprisonment. In more recent memory, Gary Gilmore and Jesse Bishop spurned the long, agonizingly slow process of appeal, and voluntarily allowed their lives to be claimed by capital punishment.[2]

California Governor George Deukmejian, a supporter of capital punishment, recently said, "Since I authored the death penalty law nearly a decade ago, 24,000 men, women, and children have been willfully killed in our state. Juries have by unanimous decisions, imposed the death penalty over 200 times—yet not one killer has paid the ultimate price. The California Supreme Court has seen to that."[3]

The governor (like so many others) completely misses the point. A basic question of fairness, or at least one of equity, is far more pertinent to the situation in California. If 24,000 citizens were indeed maliciously murdered during the time period indicated by the governor, what punishment was deemed proper for the 23,800 killers who never reached death row? The State Supreme Court of California was eminently correct in forestalling the slaughter of 200 murderers, if 23,800 others guilty of the same crime escaped the ultimate penalty—and they certainly did. This same ratio, of one death sentence imposed for each ten persons convicted of first-degree murder, also holds true on a nationwide basis.

A system which convicts only twenty percent of those committing homicides, and which sentences to death only five percent of those convicted, and only executes twenty percent of the five percent sentenced, leaves much to be desired, however staunchly one might support capital punishment.

In 20 B.C., Emperor Augustus declared himself a god, and most of his immediate successors did the same. All Christians who refused to acknowledge the Emperor as a god were summarily tried (for treason), convicted, and promptly put to death.

During the reign of Judge Roy Bean, the notorious disciplinarian of early American frontier life, the same was true for anyone convicted of capital crimes in his court. The term *all* is important here, because there were no waivers granted for age, race, sex, financial, or political status. Regardless of who they were or who they knew or how prosperous they were, *all* suffered the same fate. Those convicted under Roman law had only one avenue of appeal, to the governor of the province in which they were born, and thence to the Emperor. Under the law of the Western frontier, there was no appeal. In both instances, the verdicts were carried out within a matter of days.

Early Romans and modern-day Americans, although separated in time by some two thousand years, are merely inches apart in legal custom. Amazingly, the Romans, with all their technological ingenuity, commonly used just four methods of executing criminals: decapitation, feeding criminals to the beasts, burning at the stake, and crucifixion. Similarly, we Americans with our "advanced" civilization have approved only five forms of legal extermination.

The United States Government provides capital punishment for civilians only in cases of air piracy and for murder in drug-related cases. The U.S. Congress enacted in 1950 the Uniform Military Code of Justice, which gives military courts martial the right to execute in cases of premeditated murder. However, in 1983, the Air Force Court of Military Review declared the law unconstitutional when it overturned a death sentence for Airman Robert M. Gay. The 38-page opinion stated that the Constitution required any peacetime death sentence to "clearly articulate restrictive guidelines to aid the exercise of sentencing discretion."[4] The Army and Navy in separate rulings a year earlier had both upheld the Constitutionality of the statute.

But in the United States, thirty-seven states allow executions by hanging, firing squad, electrocution, lethal gas, or poisonous injection. Some states offer a choice to the victim; others have only one approved method. Arkansas authorizes electrocution and lethal injection. North Carolina and Wyoming use lethal injection and lethal gas. Montana and Washington use lethal injection and hanging. Oklahoma's law provides that in the event lethal injection is ruled unconstitutional, hanging or electrocution are the next methods to be employed.

The Romans had a logical explanation for each of the different methods of executions. The punishment for the crime depended on its severity and on the status of those committing it. They believed that the privileged class had a *greater* responsibility to obey the laws and should therefore be dealt with more harshly. But they also believed in death with dignity, and their forms of execution acknowledged that principle. Decapitation was viewed as the most merciful, the most noble form of capital punishment. It was reserved for the social and political elite. Death was instantaneous and painless, as befitted their status. Those holding the highest political offices were also permitted to commit suicide, and their families then allowed to keep their worldly possessions. Punishment for heretics and traitors, those who participated (intentionally or otherwise) in activities regarded by the state as seditious, was the most painful, if death can be so calibrated. The condemned were thrown into the arena to be devoured by hungry animals. Burning at the stake was usually the form of punishment for common thieves and other petty criminals. Crucifixion was considered the most disgraceful of all the forms, and was applied only to slaves, foreigners, and some political dissidents.

Approved methods of execution in the United States of America cannot be explained in any rational manner. Since most of those executed derive from only two segments of society (minorities and poor whites), we need not address here degrees of civic responsibility, or the advantages of privileged status which might make violations of law more detestable, or which might establish a method of punishment more fitting to the crime and the criminal.

The cruelty of capital punishment has not been confined to any one culture or period of time. According to a *Time Magazine* article, in ancient China an occasional penalty was "death by the thousand cuts," the slow slicing away of bits of the body. A 19th century French traveler described an equally excruciating method of execution in India during the rule of the Rajahs:

> The culprit, bound hand and foot, is fastened by a long cord, passed round his waist, to the elephant's hind leg. The latter is urged into a rapid trot through the streets of the city, and every step gives the cord a violent jerk which makes the body of the condemned wretch bound on the pavement...then his head is placed upon a stone, and the elephant executioner crushes it beneath his enormous foot.[5]

Some argue that nothing so gory could possibly happen in the United States of America. Certainly, we say, such barbarous acts were only committed by uncivilized cultures in eras long past. But, in fact, similar indecencies have occurred here and now, within relatively recent history. Vigilante lynchings were a sordid part of American life for over a century. Perhaps a lynching is more primitive than the modern-day death penalty, but it is definitely related. One lynching of infamous note happened less than forty-eight years ago in the "Show Me" state of Missouri.

On January 25, 1942, a thirty-year-old Black, Cleo Wright, was arrested for knifing Mrs. Dillard Sturgeon (white), the wife of an army sergeant, in what was described as an attempted criminal assault. The incident occurred in Sikeston, Missouri. Wright was shot three times by a local policeman, taken to the Sikeston General Hospital for medical treatment, and incarcerated at City Hall.

A mob estimated at several hundred persons surrounded the facility, smashed the door of the restroom where Wright was confined, and dragged him out. The *St. Louis Post Dispatch* wrote:

> Four other men...pulled him to the front of the building and paused there while bystanders kicked him and then dragged him feet first, his head bumping on the concrete steps, to an automobile in front of the building.
>
> Wright's knees were hooked over the rear bumper of an automobile, which was then driven slowly to the Negro residential district, stopping twice for traffic lights and pausing in front of Negro churches where services were in progress.
>
> Blanton (Scott County Prosecuting Attorney) has been unable to identify a middle-aged man who obtained a can of gasoline from a nearby filling station and poured it over the Negro's body, a youth who stuck a cigarette in the unconscious Negro's mouth, or another person who flipped a lighted match from the ground and ignited the body.
>
> ...Wright's body lay in the dirt street four hours before it was removed by a city dump truck. Even Negro undertakers refused to handle it.[6]

The people of Sikeston were not sufficiently aroused to bring the guilty before the bar of justice. Forty-one days after this barbarous act, very similar to the elephant episode, a special Scott County Grand Jury was impanelled by Circuit Judge J. C. McDowell, who instructed it, apparently tongue-in-cheek, to make "a fair and honest inquiry." Then he proceeded to admonish the jurors not to be influenced by the mass meetings protesting the lynching, and asserted, "good Negroes and white people of Sikeston are as strong for law enforcement as the good people anywhere."[7] In these kinds of cases, as usual, injustice was swift and its outcome biased. The jury foreman read the verdict in a loud voice: "We, the grand jury, find insufficient evidence to return a true bill in the matter of the mob activity at Sikeston, January 25, 1942."[7]

Even though numerous photographs were taken of the lynch mob by three photographers, the evidence was either not presented to the grand jury or was rejected during its deliberations.

The prosecuting attorney who pressed the investigation was the son of the editor of the local newspaper, *The Sikeston Standard*. His father, C. L. Blanton, wrote in his "Polecat" column on the front page of the newspaper:

> It was the feeling of those near the City Hall, where the mob formed, that it was their duty to protect the wives of those soldier boys. This should be a warning for bad Negroes to stay out of Sikeston. The mobbing of the Negro, Cleo Wright, Sunday forenoon, was an unfortunate incident, but was deserved.[8]

How thin is the invisible line between genius and insanity! What genius was required to describe the incident as unfortunate! What insanity to label it deserving! And how descriptive of the racial climate existing during this period was the fact that a major story such as this lynching, which took place 75 miles from the City Desk of the *St. Louis Post Dispatch*, appeared on page 3A, the page specifically reserved for reporting activities dealing with Negroes. The beastly treatment accorded Blacks has not changed much since the days of slavery. Daryl Cumber Dance has said:

> One of the most severe punishments awaited the slave convicted of abducting, raping, or attempting to ravish a white woman. For such an offense he might be castrated or executed....Extreme punishment was also decreed for the Negro found guilty of other crimes, such as robbery, carrying a weapon, leaving his owners' plantation without a certificate or being found on a

boat. Punishment for such offenses included...having his ear nailed to the pillory and then cut off, and being burnt in the hands in open court.[9]

The much overused argument of proponents of the death penalty is that those who take a life must be punished in like manner. One life, they say, deserves the taking of another life. This flickering sparkle of wisdom has been thoroughly discredited by Hugo Adam Bedau, Professor of Philosophy at Tufts University, who contends:

> If this principle is understood to require that punishments are unjust unless they are like the crime itself, then the principle is unacceptable. It would require us to rape rapists, torture torturers, and inflict other horrible and degrading punishments on offenders. It would require us to betray traitors and kill multiple murderers again and again, punishments impossible to inflict. Since we cannot reasonably aim to punish all crimes according to this principle, it is arbitrary to invoke it as a requirement of justice in punishing murderers with death.[10]

Dr. Bedau makes a telling point. If punishment must be designed to fit the crime, that rationale should hold true in every case before the bar if we are to deter repeat violations. Persons convicted of perjury should have their tongues cut out. Those who pick pockets should have both hands severed. "Peeping Toms" should have their eyes plucked out. This would truly be "justice for all with malice toward none."

Religious zealots seeking biblical authority for such harsh treatment do not have to look far. In the Book of *Leviticus* it states:

> Anyone who inflicts an injury on his neighbor shall receive the same in return. Limb for limb...The same injury that a man gives another shall be inflicted on him in return.[11]

This sobering bit of advice gives much comfort to proponents of an "eye for an eye." It lends further support to the philosophical position of St. Thomas Aquinas and the moral dicta of St. Paul. Those Christians who want to cite church authority for justifying capital punishment could not find any greater voices. Aquinas justified capital punishment by analogizing the relationship between an individual (a part) and society (the whole), contending that the whole must protect itself from the parts and therefore was justified in any endeavor, including capital punishment. St. Paul envisioned the death penalty as an effective deterrent. He was persuaded by a passage in *Genesis* which states: "Whoever sheds the blood of man, by man shall his blood be shed; for God made man in His own image."[12]

Thus the biblical controversy continues among religious advocates for and against the death penalty. Those who cite St. Aquinas and St. Paul derive their authority ultimately from the Old Testament. But opponents of capital punishment can now also cite chapter and verse from scripture to defend their position. It is the Book of *Ezekiel* which states: "...Thus you have spoken, saying: Our iniquities and our sins are upon us and we pine away in them: how then can we live? Say to them: As I live, saith the Lord God, I desire not the death of the wicked, but that the wicked turn from his way and live. Turn ye from your evil ways: and why will you die, O House of Israel?"[13]

III.

THE MOST INFAMOUS
EXECUTION IN HISTORY

Those who cannot remember the past are condemned to repeat it.

—George Santayana
(from *The Life of Reason, 1905-1906*, v.1)

1. The Background and History of Christ's Execution

Christians are well aware of the most infamous legal execution in recorded history, but it is not readily apparent they perceive the moral contradictions inherent in the continued application of state-approved capital punishment. Jesus Christ's murder is the most celebrated (but certainly not the only) case of governmental excessiveness in applying "criminal" penalties. It synthesizes all the arguments of those opposing the right of any government to apply the death penalty. The legal system was as terribly flawed in Roman times as it sometimes is today. Evidence presented to the court was often circumstantial, particularly if the victim was innocent, poor, and/or the member of a minority group who espoused unpopular religious, political, or social views. In addition, the judiciary was easily intimidated or subverted; then, as now, the deterrent value accruing from a prisoner's execution was minimal, and society itself sometimes suffered more than the criminal for allowing miscarriages of justice. Although the treatment afforded Jesus of Nazareth is without question an example of one of the most undeserving and unjust legal executions in the history of the world, it was by no means unique either to Roman society or to recent history; its moral implications have reverberated down through the ages, hanging like some disembodied Rock of Gibraltar around the necks of those Christians who consciously support and advocate the use of capital punishment. The torture, pain, and humiliation suffered by our Savior should be (but apparently is not) a constant reminder that the death sentence often fails catastrophically to address the moral and religious questions implicit in its application.

It is therefore imperative that we analyze from both a moral and religious view under what circumstances it might be acceptable for a person or an institution to take the life of another. War and self-defense have been offered as reasonable rationalizations for killing other humans. Hatred, envy, fear, greed, vengeance are examples of motivations which have been deemed "not acceptable" by most Christian bodies. At least three of these prompted the execution of Jesus Christ: the envy and vengeance of local Jewish leaders, and the fear of the Romans of a general Jewish uprising. In other words, Jesus was executed basically to serve local and national political needs, to stifle dissent and control the population. Sound familiar? No valid moral justification for his crucifixion has ever been suggested. The Romans regarded the teachings of Christ as an act of rebellion against the Empire. The Jewish elders believed that Jesus's death was necessary to preserve the purity of doctrine. Both assertions were and are preposterous. Indeed, it is obvious from the Scriptures that even the Roman judge (Pontius Pilate) refused to sanction the death sentence by himself. The Book of *Matthew* describes the incident:

> Now Pilate, seeing that he was doing no good, but rather that a riot was breaking out, took water and washed his hands in sight of the crowd, saying, "I am innocent of the blood of this just man; see to it yourselves." And all the people answered and said, "His blood be on us and on our children."[1]

Christians of today universally proclaim their abhorrence for the crucifixion of Jesus of Nazareth by the Romans, yet most still avidly support equally despicable state-sponsored executions of our own convicts. According to this rationale, proper judicial procedure is sufficient, once guilt has been established, to sanctify the execution process. If this is the sole criterion by which we establish the moral justification for capital punishment, then we should look back at the methods employed by the executioners of Jesus.

The legal procedures seem to have been observed in the minutest respect. Formal charges were levelled before the appropriate authorities.

The accused was arraigned and indicted according to law, informed of his charges, confronted by his accusers, and given the right to enter a plea of innocent or guilty. He was tried, convicted of blasphemy, and sentenced. The proceedings and sentence legally conformed with the laws in effect at that time. Irrespective of his innocence or guilt, Christ was *legally* executed by the appropriate judicial bodies.

Those who condone executions in twentieth-century America because legal niceties have been meticulously observed cannot at the same time object to the execution of Jesus on superfluous grounds. Notwithstanding the correctness of the legal procedure under Roman law, Christ's innocence should be sufficiently compelling in itself for his avowed followers to reject state-sanctioned execution.

Jesus was convicted of "confessing" that he was the Son of God and King of the Jews. In the eyes of his accusers, this constituted a blasphemy which, according to Jewish Scripture, was punishable by death. The High Court (the *Sanhedrin*) permitted the tragic death of an innocent man, and managed to convince the Roman Governor to sanction the execution by pointing out the potentially subversive nature of Christ's claim.

In Christ's case, scripture says that the victim rose from the dead on the third day. Who else shares these mystical powers? For all others, death is final in every sense of the word. Mistakes in the judicial process can never be rectified. Our society must bear the blame for the innocent who are wrongly executed. Procedural errors and other quirks in the American legal system all too often mean that those who are guilty are acquitted or receive reduced sentences, while too many guilty of lesser crimes (or wholly innocent of the charges levied against them) have been both convicted and executed. Only later do we find out that they were victims of judicial "mistakes." What happens to our system of justice when it is impossible to provide restitution for judicial errors? A man wrongly imprisoned can be freed and/or paid for his suffering. The man wrongly executed is dead. Ultimately, society itself is the victim, as the choice of those liable for actually being executed becomes increasingly dependent on the financial capability of the accused to hire a first-class legal defense.

Jesus of Nazareth, a Jewish citizen who was afforded all of the legal rights available to the accused of his time, was judged "guilty as charged." According to both Jewish and Roman law, his crime mandated death at the hands of the state. Let us compare the similarities between the laws under which Jesus was tried with those presently prevailing in America.

As Jesus prayed in the Garden of Gethsemane, an *eyewitness*

(Judas Iscariot) pointed him out to his captors. Immediately, he was taken to the home of the High Priest (or magistrate) for *arraignment*. There, a hurriedly assembled *Sanhedrin* (the Jewish version of the Supreme Court) interrogated him and issued the charge (*indictment*). There is nothing about this procedure that seems all that far removed from any courtroom proceeding today.

As often happens in our own courts, however, this phase of the prosecution was partially tainted. Jewish law forbade the *Sanhedrin* to meet during the Holy Season of the Passover, or at night. However, Jesus was apprehended, paraded before the court, charged, and tried during both the Passover and at night. This failure to follow procedures did not cause the verdict to be overturned.

Instead, on Friday morning, Jesus was presented before Pontius Pilate, the Governor of Judea, who officially charged him. Under Roman law, since Jesus was a native of Galilee, Pilate was required to dispatch Him to King Herod Antipas (*extradition*), the autonomous ruler of that province. There Christ was ridiculed, embarrassed, and returned to Pilate for appropriate punishment (*extradition waived*). The U.S. Supreme Court invariably returns cases to the state of origin for final disposition.

At no point in the process was there any effort critically to evaluate the allegations or to terminate the entire procedure for lack of prosecutorial evidence. This is similar to what can happen today in the United States: most of the procedure until the accused actually appears in court is a formality. Although the first stages of the process are not supposed to be adversarial, they often result in the rights of those charged being wholly ignored or even trampled upon. In other words, once the train leaves the station, it's impossible to stop its forward motion; and the person sitting in the caboose often has no idea where the train is going or how to slow it down, much less shunt it onto another track. An accused individual—*any* individual—is not permitted to present a defense before a grand jury, since that would constitute an adversarial confrontation. No witnesses can be summoned to rebut the charges made against him; such testimony *must* await a formal trial. The credibility or character of his accusers cannot be challenged under any circumstances. That too must await the impanelling of a jury, which in due course will decide the fate of the victim.

But Roman (and American) law was and is not completely devoid of compassion. Today we offer the accused felon "immunity" for turning state's evidence against other felons. A co-conspirator in an aggravated crime may escape punishment by nailing his abettor to the cross. It was also traditional for Roman governors during the Passover to let the crowd decide who of several convicted felons might be pardoned. Thus, Pilate offered to free either Barabbas, a convicted criminal, or Jesus. Those who despised and feared Jesus as a threat to their positions of power and influence used rabble-rousers to make the issue one of nationalism, with Jesus as the sacrificial lamb. According to Matthew:

> But the procurator (Pilate) addressed them, and said to them, "Which of the two do you wish that I release to you?" And they said, "Barabbas." Pilate said to them, "What then am I to do wth Jesus who is called Christ?" They all said, "Let him be crucified." The procurator said to them, "Why? What evil has he done?" But they kept crying out the more, saying, "Let him be crucified."[2]

In a self-fulfilling prophecy, the advocates of capital punishment have reaped what they have sown. The blood of tens of thousands, some of them innocent, has haunted their children and childrens' children for the last two thousand years. Pestilence, famines, wars, floods, epidemics, diseases have plagued them throughout the centuries.

When the most infamous sentence of capital punishment in history was imposed, the judge calmly and without emotion ordered the execution to take place, on a date and time certain, at the Hill of Calvary, where the victim was to be placed on a cross until officially pronounced dead.

The Man of Galilee, in the prime of his life at the age of thirty-three, suffered the ultimate punishment of "man's inhumanity to man." Clothed in a red robe, crowned wth thorns, he was nailed to the cross by his hands and feet, pierced in the side by sentries, and left to die in agony and humiliation. Whether the punishment befit the crime or the execution served to deter others inclined to rebel against the state, the crucifixion of Jesus Christ is a prime example why such barbaric treatment must be abolished.

It is inconceivable that the self-proclaimed followers of this Man should promote and support such uncivilized acts, when Jesus himself spent his entire life teaching love and forgiveness as the only viable alternatives to hate and vengeance. How those who supposedly believe in his teachings can advocate state-sanctioned judicial revenge against their fellow human beings, guilty or not, is paradoxical to the extreme.

Christians who attempt to justify capital punishment by citing the "eye for an eye" passage from the Old Testament seemingly have neither read nor understood Jesus' Sermon on the Mount, where he stated:

> But I say to you, love your enemies, do good to those who persecute and calumniate you, so that you may be children of your Father in heaven, who makes His sun to rise on the good and the evil, and sends rain on the just and the unjust.[3]

Jesus spoke of many other things during his ministry, but revenge was never among them. Articulating the differences between the old law and the new, He said:

> For I say to you that unless your justice exceeds that of the Scribes and Pharisees, you shall not enter the Kingdom of Heaven.[4]

The anger of God as often expressed in the Old Testament necessarily is described in terms relative to the human emotions of hate, wrath, revenge, fury, abomination. How else could a spiritual reaction be translated into human terms by primitive man? In *Judith*, a book of the Old Testament, it is said,

> For God will not threaten like man, nor be inflamed to anger like the Son of Man.[5]

Those who rely on the Old Testament for approval of capital punishment are flirting with intellectual disaster. The Book of *Leviticus* is filled with lists of wholly unreasonable examples of those crimes and occasions when a person should be put to death. Most certainly the Supreme Court or even the Vatican Council would today rule such decisions "arbitrary and capricious," "cruel and unusual."

However, the gruesome, uncivilized ordeal suffered in capital punishment has not deterred its implementation. One would think that followers of this most holy Man, himself victimized by a cruel, inhumane form of punishment, would have second thoughts about continuing such beastly application. How anyone aware of the savagery, pain, and suffering of crucifixion can be associated with a movement that morally sanctions the death penalty is hard to comprehend.

One of the strangest biblical justifications for capital punishment comes from the Rev. Jerry Falwell, leader of the Moral Majority, now called the Liberty Federation. He reaches further into the outer limits of incredulity than perhaps any other modern evangelist, proclaiming that Christ himself favored capital punishment. For proof of this startling absurdity, Falwell cites the crucifixion, where he says, Jesus had an excellent opportunity to speak out against capital punishment while hanging on the cross. According to Reverend Falwell, "If ever there was a platform for our Lord to condemn capital punishment, that was it. He did not."[6]

Because Jesus, whose mouth was filled with vinegar, his senses numbed, his joints aching, whose body was in a state of shock and suffering respiratory failure, did not give a long dissertation on the evils of capital punishment, Falwell believes that the Master supported state executions. Strange logic indeed, coming from an even stranger source. Of course, Rev. Falwell does not acknowledge the implications of the statement Christ did manage to utter while suffering his final excruciating minutes on the cross: "Father, forgive them; for they know not what they do."[7]

Falwell also overlooks another scene in the Bible, where a woman accused of adultery, a capital offense, is about to be stoned. Jesus says to the angry mob, "Let him who is without sin among you, be the first to cast a stone at her."[8] It's fortunate Falwell himself was not part of the mob. Death by stoning was the regular form of capital punishment for eighteen offenses prescribed in the first five books of the Old Testament, the *Pentateuch*. But the law required an eyewitness to the crime to cast the first stone. Knowing Rev. Falwell's propensity for self-interpretation of the Bible, would he have cast the first stone, even if he had *not* been an eyewitness? I wonder. The Old Testament, used by many advocates of capital punishment to bolster their arguments, actually forbade such conduct. The Book of *Numbers* states: "Whenever someone kills another, the evidence of *witnesses* is required for the execution of the murderer. The evidence of a *single* witness is not sufficient for putting a person to death."[9]

Jesus, on the other hand, clearly rejected the notion that capital punishment is an appropriate punishment by imposing an impossible condition on those contemplating the lawful execution of a felon: Being an eyewitness is insufficient justification to cast the first stone, unless you are also free from sin—and only God is free from sin. Are we any less sinful today? Who among us is all-knowing, all-wise, all-just? If the words of Jesus Christ mean anything at all, they must reaffirm the consistently-stated notion that God is the only judge and dispenser of life and death, and *man is not*.

If I have quoted excessively from scripture in attacking those who use religious sources to justify capital punishment, it is only to highlight the folly of such nonsense. For every biblical passage cited in support of governmental murder, two can be found to oppose it. If we do not truly believe in the possibility of human redemption, that same redemption promised by Jesus Christ to all who have faith, we are not Christians, we are barbarians masquerading in Christian skins, no better (and possibly worse, in our hypocrisy) than the misguided politicians who 2,000 years ago executed our Savior. And I for one would prefer to err, if err I must, on the side of love, of truth, of justice, yes, even on the side of hope.

2. The Inherent Cruelty of Execution

We cannot begin to imagine the horror and suffering experienced by those who are executed. Some pain is so excruciating that it cannot be described even by those who have experienced it. Marcello Craveri, in his book *The Life of Jesus*, attempts to portray the last hours of those being crucified:

> At nightfall, as their law required, the Roman legionaries performed the breaking of the legs (*crucifragium*), if the condemned men were still alive, lest someone take advantage of the darkness to set them free. To judge by the Gospel of John, this was not done to Jesus, because he was dead. But a legionary thrust a lance into his side, and blood mixed with water came forth. Christian legend has even given this soldier a name: Longinus. Taken in actuality from the Greek (*longche*), which means "lance," the so-called proper name simply means "the lancer." The lance probably did not strike hard enough to go through the abdomen of Jesus and reach his heart, despite tradition, which questions whether the blow did not hasten his last moments. It was only a small incision in his side, to make certain that the condemned man was really dead and not merely unconscious. The water that came out of the wound with the blood was lung fluid oozing through because of circulatory stagnation.
>
> Death came from other causes. Many students, especially physicians, have tried to isolate them: Ac-

cording to Seriog Marigo, the death of Jesus was brought on by an embolism that closed off an artery. Verut, LeBec, Giovannie Judica Cordiglia, and others blame instead a traumatic shock and a sudden syncope as a result of the intensification of pain. R. Whithaker suggests a rupture of the myocardium caused by a sharp movement, perhaps an effort to change position.

All these hypotheses, however, envisage an unforeseen death from exceptional causes probably peculiar to cases of this kind. In them is an attempt to justify the debatable version of the facts offered by the Gospels: the three-hour stages of the death, the three-day period of the judgment, death, and resurrection, etc. Even as long ago as the time of Origen, students of the subject were astounded at the swiftness of the death of Jesus and considered it a miracle, for it was well-known that the agony of the crucified never ended in less than two days. Hynek points out that death in such cases occurs through the slow development of tetanic cramps brought on by spasmodic muscular contractions; the cramps start in the strained muscles of the forearm, then extend into the whole arm, the upper body, the abdomen, the legs. At the same time, Franco La Cava and Joseph Hammer say, the position of the body impedes the circulation of the blood and a progressive carboxyhemia is produced, terminating in a asystrolic heart block. That death is extremely slow is emphasized by Binet-Sangle, Kurt Berna, and others. The contraction of the muscles and the enforced immobility impose an enormous burden on the heart; its pulse is inexorably slowed and the blood stagnates in the capillary vessels. Poisoned by the waste matter that the heart can no longer eliminate, the muscles are affected by tonic spasms, which cause unbearable spastic phenomena. As a consequence of the dimunition in circulation, the blood carries progressively less oxygen to the lungs but is increasingly contaminated by carbon dioxide, and the victim feels that he is suffocating.[10]

Crucifixion was without doubt a horrible way to die. The Latin word *excruciatus*, from which the later English word derives, was often used to describe the pain of hanging on the cross. It was customary for Roman soldiers to severely beat victims before driving the six-inch spikes through their hands, wrists, and feet.

Yet, if any one incident illuminates the forebearance, forgiveness, and charity demonstrated by the life of Jesus, it is the scene at the Garden of Gethsemane. When the mob came to take him to his ultimate execution, an end he clearly foresaw, one of the Apostles took out his sword and cut off a soldier's ear. Jesus disarmed his disciple and put the ear back where it belonged.

In ordering His followers to sheath their swords, Christ stated:

> Put back thy sword into its place; for all those who take the sword will perish by the sword. Or dost thou suppose that I cannot entreat my Father, and He will even now furnish me with more than twelve legions of angels?[11]

Today, however, a victim cannot call even on twelve "good men and true" to defend his right to life. Our government now requires potential jurors to swear to their belief in death as a fitting retribution for capital crimes. Those expressing personal convictions in opposition to capital punishment are automatically rejected. This is a sad commentary on a society which outwardly expresses its repugnance at indiscriminate killing, and proudly proclaims such inalienable rights as "life, liberty and the pursuit of happiness."[12]

After Jesus had been seized, he was taken before the *Sanhedrin* (the Jewish High Court). The "King of the Jews" was found guilty of high crimes, but the Jewish High Court doubted its authority to impose a sentence. Had Jesus only been found guilty of blasphemy, the law was clear: the *Sanhedrin* was clearly empowered to impose death either by stoning or strangulation.

The fact that Jesus was taken before Pontius Pilate indicates the political nature of the charges against him. In retrospect, this charade parallels many present-day deficiencies in our own legal process. False witnesses, dubious charges, sensationalism, and pervasive political influence exerted by pillars of the community are as evident in the twentieth century as they were in 33 A.D.

For twenty-five centuries critics have debated the morality of state-inflicted capital punishment, but not until the last two centuries have abolitionists gained enough strength to affect its usage even marginally. Prior to that time, public arguments were confined to which method was the most cruel, and therefore, according to the "wisdom" of the day, most effective in deterring crime. These apologists seem to have ignored the fact that capital crimes have continued unabated throughout history. History also reveals mankind's innate ability to devise schemes of extreme torture, although the rigors of crucifixion (when compared to other forms) seem overpowering.

Royalty and nobility were not immune: Sir Thomas More, King Richard II, King Charles I, and Queen Marie Antoinette were executed as object lessons for the masses. Public spectacles were designed specifically to accompolish two purposes: torture and humiliation. One of the most publicized executions in history was that of Damien, the unsuccessful assassin of Louis XIV. According to an article in *Time* magazine, government agents made a public spectacle of the execution:

> His flesh was torn with red-hot pincers, his right hand was burned with sulfur, his wounds were drenched with molten lead. His body was drawn and quartered by four horses, his parts were set afire and his ashes scattered to the winds. The execution was accomplished before a large crowd.[13]

During this period, France was considered the epitome of refinement, culture, and Christian civility. These attributes apparently meant little when considering how intemperately Frenchmen treated other Frenchmen. Although Damien was unsuccessful in killing Louis XIV, the latter's descendant, King Louis XVI, was guillotined on January 21, 1793, to be followed on October 16th by Queen Marie Antoinette.

The mass amnesia of Christians concerning the lesson of history is extremely puzzling. Damien was just one of the many victims who have suffered legalized death at the hands of supposedly devout believers. Yet, we see in modern America no public outcry for abolition of capital punishment, only for its restoration. The various adherents of Jesus Christ, Muhammad, or Buddha are unique only in their devotion to different forms of cruel and unusual punishment.

In past centuries, Germans placed victims in large kettles filled with water and boiled them alive. Vietnamese prisoners of war were tortured to death by placing poisoned bamboo sticks under their fingernails.

Some societies have imposed the ultimate penalty through systematic starvation; others, presumably more enlightened, have preferred forced feeding. Efficient Nazi exterminators used gas ovens and showers. American Indians abandoned their malcontents in the desert to die of heat and thirst. State-sanctioned death in the United States today is no less merciless than forms used in yesteryear by other countries. It's still just as barbaric and inexcusable.

The crisis of mass execution in the United States is now upon us. Over two thousand persons now await the gallows. Some of our people have spoken out against this outrage; most have not. As Dante wrote, "The hottest spots in hell are reserved for those who refused to speak out in times of moral crisis."[14] Those Christians grappling with this moral crisis must weigh the fruits of temporary satisfaction and instant revenge with the possibility of an infinitely more final judgment of everlasting damnation.

If the Son of God, the Founder of Christianity, can be illegally arrested, falsely charged, improperly tried, erroneously convicted, and brutally executed, then so can anyone else, even in these so-called "enlightened" times. If this fact fails to steer his avowed followers away from capital punishment, then all I can say, to opponents and proponents alike is: "Dear Lord, verily, let us pray." One can only hope that the Jerry Falwells of this world will not reply: "Let their blood be on us and on our children."

IV.

THE DEATH PENALTY AS A DETERRENT

Reason is on our side, feeling is on our side, and experience is on our side. In those states where punishment by death is abolished, the mass of capital crime has yearly a progressive decrease. Let this fact have its weight.

—Victor Hugo

1. The Fallacy of the Deterrent Theory

State government is as successful in using capital punishment to deter crime as it is in training jackrabbits to retrieve newspapers. The threat of death serves as no more of a deterrence to hardened criminals than do ordinary door locks to professional burglars. The scientific evidence, as reflected in hundreds of studies by noted sociologists and criminologists, points to capital punishment as a neglible element in keeping others from committing similar crimes. Furthermore, common sense tells us that three hundred years of American experimentation with capital punishment has not *decreased* the number (or violence) of capital crimes one whit; if anything, such crimes have *increased* dramatically since the reimposition of the death penalty in the 1980s. Common sense would further instruct us (if anyone were listening) that our current criminal justice system is simply not working, on whatever basis or by whatever standard we might wish to measure it.

The fear of being detected, arrested, and sentenced is *not* a primary concern of most career criminals. Who says so? The professionals do: the police, the judges, the prosecutors, the criminologists, and, most importantly, the criminals themselves. However, most murders are committed by laymen or amateurs, *not* by career criminals, and such individuals almost never pause to consider the consequences, if they even understand them. The motivating causes of their crimes are spontaneous rage and passion.

Psychologists have long stated that the degree to which judicial punishment is effective depends directly on the ability of the state to carry out uniform methods of application. The mandating of a harsh penalty in and of itself has a lesser impact on deterring criminal acts than generally demonstrating resolve for punishing the culprits in some form—and then making certain that they are, in fact, caught and punished. If a central authority merely introduces repressive measures without simultaneously ensuring universal justice, the opposite will result. The greatest weapon to contain those who would commit acts of violence against others is making certain that a large percentage of those individuals will actually be subjected to coercive punishment or treatment, of whatever kind.

Our current system of justice is notable for its *in*justice, for patting certain rich and influential persons on the wrist while throwing the book at others, with the vast majority of all felons never being apprehended at all. It is no wonder, then, that the potential criminal is left with the sense that, for the most part, *crime does pay.* Those who abuse the rules must know that punishment will be quickly and universally applied *to them* and to all other violators.

In the debate surrounding capital punishment, much of the focus has been placed on the issue of capital punishment as a supposedly effective deterrent to crime, particularly the crime of murder. Various statistical methods have been employed by both sides to answer this question. The results have been inconclusive. No study, not even those employing the most sophisticated statistical techniques, has ever satisfactorily proved or disproved the effectiveness of the death penalty as a deterrent.

Simply stated, "deterrence" refers to a circumstance in which an individual refrains from an act because he or she perceives a risk of punishment for the act and fears that punishment. According to arguments put forward by proponents of capital punishment, people fear death more than anything else, and death is therefore the most effective possible deterrent.

This assertion contradicts basic religious tenets of most faiths, which hold that life on Earth is a transition period necessary for union with God in heaven. Espousing an unnatural fear of death injects a misleading element into religious discourse. Those who truly believe in the dignity of all life and a respect for all humans, whatever their religious tenets, are not usually the ones facing capital punishment judgments. The victims of capital punishment are individuals who have never considered death, its ramifications, or its meaning. For Christians to perceive death as a tragic moment in human experience while at the same time preaching that it is the only opportunity for reunion with the Creator, bewilders those who are neither Christian nor atheist. Deliberately and prematurely terminating human life is understandable to some, but not to those who are aware of the Christian abhorrence of suicide. If death is so fearful, why do people commit suicide? If capital punishment must exist to rid society of those who may potentially engage in the murder and mayhem, why should good Christians object to those who take their own lives? Have not these individuals condemned themselves, one might ask, in the same way that criminals have? Are we upset merely by the disruption of our little peaceful existences? Is it not hypocritical to attempt to dissuade the potential suicide from his or her own self-immolation while simultaneously as a society pulling the switch that fries the convicted felon? If the suicide's life is sacred in the eyes of God, is not the criminal's?

The doctrine of deterrence and its importance in the capital punishment controversy have been described as follows:

> ...by far the most common way to employ a punishment as a preventative of crime is to adopt a sufficiently severe penalty so as to compel general obedience out of fear of the consequences of disobedience—the classic doctrine of deterrence. Even though deterrence cannot override every other concern in formulating a rational penal philosophy, there is no doubt that the death penalty's efficacy as a deterrent is the major factual issue in dispute between abolitionists and retentionists.[1]

The deterrence doctrine is based on the proposition that murder results from rational thought processes; i.e., that potential murderers acknowledge the existence of the death penalty and the likelihood of its being applied to them, and that they decide to murder or not depending on the risks and benefits of committing the specific crime. It is this proposition that has been the target of particular criticism. Critics of the deterrence doctrine argue that many, if not most, murders are crimes of passion or provocation—not premeditation or deliberation—committed by irrational or mentally unbalanced individuals. Such individuals, it is argued, are either incapable of calculating the costs and benefits of their actions (and, therefore, incapable of being deterred by the death penalty), or just don't care.[2] On the other hand, proponents of the doctrine argue that even if most murders are crimes of passion, this does not mean that capital punishment cannot be a deterrent. They argue that it is precisely because of the severe penalties prescribed for murder that murders tend to be committed by those unable rationally to weigh the costs and benefits. The result, say such theorists, is that potential murderers who are actually deterred do not appear in crime statistics.[3]

However, there is no way to determine how many murders result from acts of passion or provocation, and how many are premeditated or deliberate. The best statistics available are those published in the FBI's yearly *Uniform Crime Reports*, which attempt to categorize murders according to circumstances or motive. These statistics are not broken down by states. The most recent figures available are provided in Table A (see the Appendix).

The chart indicates that nearly thirty-eight percent of reported murders in 1986 involved some type of argument. This could be viewed as evidence that murder is largely an irrational act. However, there are problems in relying on such figures. First, the circumstances or motivations behind the crime are reported by local police, often based on evidence provided by observers. There is no way to determine if the reported circumstances accurately represent the true facts of each case. More importantly, the FBI's categories are broad and somewhat vague. It is impossible from these antiseptic figures to determine whether a particular murder, even when associated with an argument, was premeditated or the result of an emotional outburst. Likewise, it would be impossible to know whether a felony murder (i.e., a murder committed during the course of another felony) was premeditated or the result of fear or panic. Furthermore, nearly thirty-three percent of the cases fall into the "other" or "unknown" motive or circumstances category.

Before discussing the major studies of the deterrent effect of capital punishment, some general observations should be made. Firstly, what these studies have attempted to measure is the *marginal* and not the *absolute* deterrent effect of capital punishment. In other words, the question dealt with is not whether the death penalty deters *at all*, but whether it is a more effective deterrent than imprisonment. Secondly, the studies have been confined almost exclusively to the death penalty for criminal homicide. Therefore, even if a study finds that capital punishment is not an effective deterrent for that crime, this does not mean the death penalty could not be a superior deterrent for other crimes. And thirdly, the deterrent effect of the death penalty has been tested only indirectly. No one has devised a way to count or estimate directly the number of persons who have been deterred from criminal homicide by fear of capital punishment. If every study of deterrence and the death penalty were reviewed, the same conclusion would be reached—the real deterrent effect of capital punishment is unknown, and possibly unknowable.

2. Comparisons of Homicide Rates

One way to study the possible deterrent effect of the death penalty is to compare the homicide rates of death penalty jurisdictions with the homicide rates of non-death penalty jurisdictions. Karl Schuessler did this for five selected years between 1928 and 1949, and found the homicide rate for states with the death penalty to be *two to three times higher* than for states without the death penalty![4] Table I (see the Appendix) gives the homicide rate per 100,000 population from the FBI's *Uniform Crime Reports* for states with and without the death penalty in 1985.

As the chart indicates, the states with no death penalty had a lower average murder rate than those with a death penalty (4.75 per 100,000 population as compared to 6.8 per 100,000). However, such a simple comparison can be misleading. For instance, using an overall average murder rate for each of the two groups of states obscures the fact that the states within each group have a broad range of murder rates. / For non-death penalty states the range is from 1.0 (North Dakota) to 11.2 (Michigan) murders per 100,000 people. For death penalty states the range is from 1.8 (South Dakota) to 13.0 (Texas) murders per 100,000 people. / Not only is the range of murder rates broad within each group, but there is also a good deal of overlap between rates in the two groups. If this test conclusively proved the effect of the presence or absence of a death penalty statute on murder rates, one would expect that there would be a more substantial difference in overall average murder rates between the two groups of states.

Another reason why this comparison can be misleading is that it rests on the obviously oversimplified assumption that no factors other than the death penalty affect a state's murder rate. The death penalty/non-death penalty grouping obviously ignores socio-cultural differences among the states. As one critic has pointed out:

> The obvious socio-cultural differences between the abolition states and the states in the South, where homicide rates are several times higher...almost cer-

tainly obliterates whatever effects are attributable to the relevant variable, the different mode of punishment.[5]

To meet such objections, more sophisticated statistical investigations were conducted, primarily by Thorsten Sellin. He examined groups of contiguous states, each group containing at least one state with a capital punishment statute ("retentionist") and one state which had abolished capital punishment ("abolitionist"). He attempted to match states that were as nearly alike socio-economically and demographically as possible. He then compared the rates for murder and non-negligent manslaughter over the period 1920 to 1958, and found that the homicide rates of retentionist states did not generally differ over time from the homicide rates of abolitionist states. Sellin concluded:

> Within each group of states having similar social and economic conditions and populations, it is impossible to distinguish the abolition state from the others....The inevitable conclusion is that executions have no discernible effect on homicide death rates.[6]

Other studies using the same approach have arrived at similar results.[7]

This work by Sellin and others has been criticized on several grounds. First, the use of the existence of a death penalty statute to identify states as retentionist or abolitionist has been deemed misleading, because the relevant variable should be the *extent* of use of capital punishment. For example, it has been pointed out that in many of Sellin's "retentionist" states, capital punishment was rarely imposed, if ever, and that therefore the actual risk of execution was negligible.[8] Sellin's analysis also has been criticized as "inevitably subjective" in its selection of states to be compared[9]:

> The similar areas are not similar enough; the periods are not long enough; many social differences and changes, other than the abolition of the death penalty, may account for the variation (or lack of) in homicide rates with and without, before and after abolition; some of these social differences and changes are likely to have affected homicide rates.[10]

Finally, Sellin's matching technique has been criticized as ignoring a possible "feedback" response of punishment policies to homicide rates; in other words, a high or rising homicide rate may have led a particular state to institute the death penalty, and a low or falling rate may have led others to abolish it. Therefore, the retentionist states would tend to have higher homicide rates, and a simple correlation of capital punishment and homicide rates would only see the relationship between high murder levels and the existence of the statute.[11]

Table II (see the Appendix) provides a breakdown of homicide rates for 1985, for abolitionist and retentionist states within each federal judicial circuit. Federal circuits were chosen because they are easily recognizable and are not subject to manipulation, and therefore avoid the subjectivity in the selection of contiguous states for which Sellin was criticized. A breakdown by federal circuit does not, however, respond to the other major criticisms of Sellin's work, most of which can be addressed only through the use of more sophisticated statistical techniques. Table II also provides only a cross-sectional analysis: *i.e.*, an analysis of data for a single time period. Unlike Sellin's analysis, it does not consider trends over time.

The conclusions that can be drawn from this table are subject to the same limitations that apply to Sellin's contiguous state analysis. To the extent that there is no socio-demographic similarity among states within a circuit, the differences shown between the murder rates of abolitionist and retentionist states lose some of their merit. The possible feedback response of punishment policy to homicide rate is not considered, nor is the fact that variables other than the death penalty may affect a state's murder rate. Like the previous tables, Table II is inconclusive as to the deterrent effect of the death penalty.

Another analysis undertaken by Sellin examined changes in homicide rates in eleven states which abolished and later reintroduced the death penalty. From the examination he concluded that "there is no evidence that the abolition of the death penalty generally causes an increase in criminal homicides or that its reintroduction is followed by a decline."[12] Sellin himself recognized that the data from some of the states was "admittedly poor," and that so few states had changed policies in this manner that the evidence was of questionable probative value.

Table III (see the Appendix) presents data on murder rates in states that abolished the death penalty during the 1970s. The Supreme Court's many decisions regarding death penalty laws during this period resulted in a number of states having their laws invalidated or being forced to repeal existing death penalty statutes. However, most of these jurisdictions quickly instituted new laws to conform to court rulings. Eight states—Kansas, Massachusetts, Missouri, New Jersey, New Mexico, Colorado, Ohio and South Dakota—repealed their death penalty statutes and did not reinstitute them before 1979. The state of Washington repealed its death penalty statute in 1973 and reinstituted it in July of 1976. Table III provides the murder rates for these states for the years 1971-1979.

The trends over time suggest no clear pattern. It would be very difficult to argue from the information in this table that the abolition of the death penalty had any significant impact on the murder rates in these states. In Massachusetts, New Hampshire and Washington, the average murder rates for the years when the death penalty was in effect are higher than when it was not in effect. In New Jersey and Missouri (where the death penalty was in effect for one year), and in Kansas (where it was in effect for two years) during the period of investigation, the years without the death penalty have higher average murder rates than the years with the death penalty. No inferences can be made from these findings. These trends do not show a consistent pattern across states. This suggests that factors other than the death penalty are important in affecting the changes in murder rates in these states.

3. The Work of Isaac Ehrlich and His Critics

The "cross tabulations" or matched sample technique used by Sellin in his comparison of states with and without the death penalty has important limitations. In particular, this approach does not take into consideration (*i.e.*, it does not "control" for) all important factors that might affect murder rates. The matched sample comparison does not consider factors other than abolition or retention of the death penalty. For example, in the comparison of contiguous states, states are matched by geographical location, but the number of handguns available per capita is not considered. This and similar factors could be important elements in explaining differences in murder rates.

As a result of such limitations, a number of analysts have used multivariate statistical techniques to explore the deterrence hypothesis. The majority of these studies rely on a technique called multiple regression analysis. In this type of study the analyst uses an algebraic equation that estimates the effect of a particular variable or variables (the independent variables) on a variable of interest (the dependent variable). In the case of the deterrence hypothesis the variable of interest is the likelihood of murder; the independent variables in the numerous regression analyses have varied with the study.

One of the most sophisticated and controversial investigations of the deterrence question employing multiple regression analysis was done by Isaac Ehrlich.[13] In his analysis Ehrlich reported that "an additional execution per year over the period in question may have resulted, on average in seven to eight fewer murders."[14] Ehrlich's conclusion was based on an analysis of yearly information collected for the years 1933-1969 for the entire United States. In his analysis of this data he factored in a number of independent social and demographic variables, including labor force participation rate, estimated per capita income, unemployment rates, and the proportion of the population in the age group 14 to 24. Ehrlich chose these variables because he believed that each may have contributed to the increase in murder rates over the time period examined. These variables were in addition to those more closely linked to such law enforcement processes as arrest and conviction rates.

Although Ehrlich's statistical formulation incorporated a number of variables never before considered, his critics have still argued that his results lack "robustness." That is, other researchers using slightly different but similar data, different time periods, or different statistical tests have been unable to duplicate his results. Criticism has been directed at both the substantive and methodological aspects of his work. On the substantive level, some have attacked the validity of his assumptions about deterrence, while on the methodological level, they have questioned the adequacy of his statistical analysis.

The first set of criticisms revolve around the issue of what is the most appropriate way to define and measure deterrence. Some critics argue that Ehrlich's analysis excludes important elements that might explain changes in the murder rate: for example, the decline in the length of prison sentences during the 1960s.[15] Others contend that there is no known way to determine all the elements that should be included:

> There is no reason to think that economics or any other
> discipline has yet identified the determinants of the
> murder rate with enough confidence to rely on results
> obtained from regression analysis.[16]

Most of the criticisms of the Ehrlich study are criticisms of his statistical method. While the substantive criticisms could be viewed as placing his study in perspective—*i.e.*, limiting its implications, but recognizing it as an indicator of the lack of agreement on the theory of deterrence—the methodological critics question the analytical soundness of the study. The precise nature of these criticisms is highly technical, but most of them have at least some merit.[17]

The Ehrlich study and the criticism it has generated have resulted in a number of other attempts to test the deterrence hypothesis using multivariate statistical techniques. These other studies in general can be divided into two groups: those attempting to measure a deterrent effect over time, as Ehrlich did (time series analysis), and those attempting to measure a deterrent effect at a single point in time (cross-sectional analysis).

4. Time Series Analyses

According to one reviewer of the literature on time series analysis:

> Of six additional analyses of time series data on the United States (in addition to the Ehrlich study), only one has attributed significant deterrent effects to capital punishment. That one analysis is extremely flawed; in general it can show no significant deterrent effects from capital punishment. This conclusion is based almost entirely on empirical work. The critics of Ehrlich do not offer an explicit alternative theoretical model explaining the determinants of murder.[18]

Before reviewing the most important of the time series studies, it is necessary to note that failure to prove a significant deterrent effect with statistical analysis does not imply that there is no deterrent effect. It does show, however, that attempts to demonstrate it have been unsuccessful thus far. The possibility remains that an alternative model of deterrence could be proposed, and if that model were widely accepted by knowledgeable analysts, it would be possible to prove that capital punishment deters murder. No such alternative has been proposed in the literature to date.

The work of Passell and Taylor used data very similar to that used by Ehrlich, but excluded certain years from the analysis, specifically, 1963-1969. With those years excluded, Passell and Taylor found that Ehrlich's deterrent effect became statistically insignificant; that is, the difference might be wholly attributable to chance.[19] Between 1963-1969, there were only forty-six executions in this country, less than 1.5 percent of all executions for the period 1930-1969. This low execution rate, along with a steady increase in the murder rate over this time period,[20] are the likely explanation for the difference between the Passell and Taylor results and the Ehrlich results. In other words, Ehrlich's data reflects the inverse relationship between executions and murder during the 1960s, while Passell and Taylor's findings are not influenced by this fact. Whether to include or exclude these years is a debatable question. If one accepts the statistical notion of "robustness" (explained above), subperiods within a longer time period should have the same characteristics as the longer period. The Passell/Taylor analysis could thus indicate that Ehrlich's deterrence model is not statistically robust.

In 1976, James Yunker published a study which supported the Ehrlich findings. The Yunker study analyzed data for the 1960-1972 time period. His regression model showed that "one execution will deter 156 murders."[21] These results have been severely criticized. Yunker employed only two independent variables—unemployment rate and execution rate—and critics have argued that his regression analysis was overly simplistic. His failure to include additional variables probably accounts for the large discrepancy between his results and those of Ehrlich and Passell and Taylor. Critics have also argued that Yunker's selection of the 1960-1972 period focused on a time when there was an increasing murder rate and a low number of executions. Such a time period lends itself to proof of the deterrence doctrine.

No researchers using a time series analysis other than Ehrlich and Yunker have found that there is a deterrent effect from executions.

5. Cross-Sectional Analyses

Cross-sectional analysis does not examine the effects of variables over time, but looks instead at their effect at a given point in time. All the time series studies discussed above examined data for the United States as a whole. As a result, data from executing states was combined with the data from non-executing states. By using cross-sectional analysis, the researcher can refine his results by distinguishing between executing and non-executing states, and also by using additional variables not available over time.

Peter Passell, analyzing data for forty-one states in 1950 and forty-four states in 1960, concluded that "students of capital punishment must look elsewhere for evidence concerning deterrence. We know of no reasonable way of interpreting the cross-section data that would lend support to the deterrence hypothesis."[22] He did find, however, that five variables—conviction rates, average prison sentences, poverty, age and rural-urban migration—plus an additional variable for southern states, did account for a great deal of the variations in murder rate from state to state. Passell admitted that it could not be proved that executions do *not* serve as a deterrent to murder, but concluded that "Proof is simply beyond the capacities of empirical social science."[23]

Brian Forst examined the changes in murder rates from 1960-1970, and like Passell found no support for the hypothesis that capital punishment deters murder. In fact, he went further than Passell, asserting that "it is erroneous to view capital punishment as a means of reducing the homicide rate."[24] Forst found that the most important factors affecting the change in murder rates over the ten-year period were murder conviction rate, economic variables, race, and the overall increase in crime during the 1960s.[25] Forst concluded with regard to punishment that certainty rather than severity was the relevant factor:

> The apparent strength of the incarceration rate variable and apparent weakness of the execution rate and term of imprisonment variables as deterrents to homicide lend some support to Cesare Becarria's two-hundred-year-old suggestion that certainty of punishment deters more effectively than its severity....[26]

Ehrlich contributed an important study to cross-section literature as well as the time series literature, performing a cross-sectional analysis for the years 1940 and 1950, distinguishing between executing and non-executing states. As with his earlier analysis, Ehrlich used sophisticated statistical techniques and once again found a deterrent effect. This time he estimated that 20-24 murders would have been deterred by one execution.[27]

Dale Cloninger used a model which distinguished between southern and non-southern states.[28] Like Ehrlich, Cloninger found a deterrent effect based on data for forty-eight states in 1960. However, his estimates varied significantly from those of Ehrlich. Whereas Ehrlich found that 20-24 murders would have been deterred by one execution in 1950, Cloninger's estimate for 1960 was that 560 murders would have been deterred. The difference between these two results is attributable to the use of different variables and the different time period analyzed.

William Boyes and Lee McPheters performed another study using data for 1960, the same year as that used by Cloninger. They concluded that "There seems to be no independent deterrent effect of capital punishment for violent crime, when probability of imprisonment, length of prison term, and other control variables are included in the model."[29] They further noted that "these results do suggest that the threat of imprisonment does deter both homicide and rape."[30] The difference between the Boyes and McPheters findings and those of Cloninger again is attributable to the use of different variables in the analysis. The different results achieved in all these studies underscores the importance of variable selection.

As with the multivariate time-series analyses, the multivariate cross-section analyses lack consistency in their findings. The empirical results are greatly influenced by the statistical design and by the variables included for examination.

One reviewer of the deterrence literature has said of this entire body of work:

> There are glaring gaps in the scientific literature on the deterrent efficacy of capital punishment....Given the gaps in the literature, candid social scientists can contribute only one general observation to the great debate over the death penalty. That observation reduces to this statement: So little is known about the deterrent or other preventive effects of capital punishment (if any) that the decision to abolish or to reinstate the punishment can only rest on principles of justice (the retributive doctrine in particular) that are beyond scientific assessment.[31]

Research conducted by Scott H. Decker, of the Center for Metropolitan Studies Administration of Justice, University of Missouri at Saint Louis, and Carol W. Kohfeld, the Department of Political Studies, University of Missouri at Saint Louis, was limited to the state of Missouri over a forty-seven-year period. They addressed the methodological issues which they contend have "clouded the results of past empirical deterrence studies." They maintained that by using a single state, concerns over comingled effects were successfully addressed, by "overcoming the inferential difficulty of data aggregated to the national level to determine whether observed results occur in one or fifty states." They also examined the impact of executions on homicide rates after one or two years to determine if there was a lagged impact; and included demographic and socio-economic characteristics in their study, researching factors such as effect of age and sex, urbanization, and unemployment rates. And lastly, but more importantly, they measured and compared homicide rates in three periods of time:

1. when the death penalty was in force and executions occurred,
2. when the death penalty was in force and no executions occurred, and
3. when there was no death penalty.

Their conclusion was as follows:

> In the current analysis a time series of 48 years for the state of Missouri was employed to assess the deterrent effect of executions. No deterrent effect could be determined from any of four analyses—graphed eras, difference of mean homicide rates for threat, use, and abolition periods, correlations, and a multivariate analysis. The implications of this research are unequivocal— those who support the use of the death penalty for Missouri do so solely on retributive grounds.[32]

6. Cheap Life in a Cheaper Society

These studies conducted by criminologists, political scientists, and sociologists have largely concluded that even in highly publicized cases, involving specific geographical areas, homicides have not diminished appreciably during the periods just before or immediately following publicized executions. Homicides are no more frequent in states which have abolished capital punishment than in those who still employ it. Lives and property are no more at risk in such areas than in any other with comparable demographic features.

If, as its proponents claim, the main purpose of capital punishment is to deter potential criminals from committing their crimes, we do not see such a result in published statistics correlating criminous activity with severity of punishment. Proponents have argued that death, being the most fearful punishment that can be imposed on man, is also the most effective deterrent. If this is true, it should be a relatively simple matter to demonstrate a relationship between its present-day application and some marked decrease in violent crimes which merit the punishment. Reasonable people, so the argument goes, will fear the ultimate punishment sufficiently to give up their criminal careers. But most murderers are not reasonable people, or even sane people, by the usual societal norms, and the reasons why they commit their crimes have little to do with the laws of man or nature. Such people are unlikely to be swayed by the miniscule potential of their legal execution, and are far more likely to fear violent deaths at the hands of their "business" colleagues.

Clifford Futch is typical of the average death row prisoner: poor and uneducated. He was sentenced to die for killing another inmate in a Pennsylvania prison while serving a life sentence. Perhaps he has articulated the reality better than most:

> When the D.A. said he was gonna try for the death penalty on me, it was a shock...it had never registered on me that I could be in this position, too.[33]

Futch admitted that the only time he had ever thought much about the death penalty was when he saw an old James Cagney movie portraying an execution. If our general knowledge of capital punishment is derived largely from old Class B flicks, no wonder so few fear its consequences.

Reliable scientific information indicates that:

a. the majority of murders in the United States are neither deliberate and premeditated, but crimes of passion and provocation, including immediate relatives killing other relatives (especially spouses), neighbors in disputes with other neighbors, arguments on streets with total strangers;

b. seldom, if ever, do those who plan to take the life of another stop to consider the consequences of getting caught and being punished;

c. very few persons who commit homicides are actually executed, and those executions which do take place are handled so quietly and privately that the deterrence value is limited.

The use of fear to deter criminal conduct seems to contradict current religious thought. At one time, most church leaders believed that the most effective means of converting pagans and keeping their followers faithful to the church was through the employment of fear. Fire-and-brimstone sermons, the threat of eternal damnation, conversions and condemnations—these were the order of the day. Today such stern doctrinarian fantasies have gradually been acknowledged as counterproductive in an educated society, except among the most extreme fundamentalist groups. Most present-day religious leaders have stated that love and reason, not hate and fear, are the more persuasive elements in saving souls. Theologians and missionaries preach the rewards of good conduct rather than the fear of ultimate penalties for bad conduct: everlasting life in Heaven with the love of God, as opposed to eternal damnation in Hell with the Devil and his minions.

This same trend has transformed modern psychology. For many years it was standard procedure to modify the actions of children by threatening them with ghosts or bogeymen, or, more practically, with the use of corporal punishment, such as the switch or strap. Then came solitary confinement, standing in corners, going to bed without dinner. An array of punishments based on fear was developed throughout the years. At least in part due to their limited deterrence values, these strategies have been largely discarded, and acknowledged by most experts as extremely damaging to the child's development (in fact, such abuse is believed by many sociologists to be a major contributor to the delineation of the "criminal" mind).

In place of such measures, modern-day psychologists, parents, and family counselors prefer such vastly different methods as reason and love in dealing with children. Teaching people, even "little" people, to understand why certain behavior is unfair to others seems to produce better results for most people. Formulating a code of ethics based on respect for the rights of others rather than on the fear of being punished also results in a much saner (and less criminous) society.

Admittedly, the acts of little children are not the same as those of hardened criminals. Surely, the need to discipline tiny tots cannot be equated to the necessity of properly punishing hardened incorrigibles. I do not suggest that we let such men and women loose on society, once they have established the patterns of their lives. All would agree that those who are menaces to society should forfeit their rights to freely mingle with law-abiding citizens. They must be segregated from the general populace forever, or for whatever length of time it takes make them safe for society. Killing them is not the only solution. It's not even the most effective solution.

The present system of trying to intimidate and frighten those who engage in anti-social acts has failed to achieve its goal by any standard of measurement. One recent study indicates that the death penalty may in fact induce even more crime. Bowers and Pierce, of the Center for Applied Social Research at Northeastern University, found that criminous activity in the state of Massachusetts between 1907-1963 actually increased after each execution at an average of two homicides per month *more* in the period immediately following the event. This finding held true even when other possibly relevant factors were accounted for, including seasonality, the effects of war, and social trends of the time.

The two authors suggested that the executions may actually have devalued and cheapened life in the public's eye, because such events are viewed by the public as akin to human sacrifice. In addition, public executions (not to mention the fictionalization and glorification of crime on television) have a tendency to demonstrate murder as an appropriate (if final) way of settling disputes.

At the very least, the burden of proof must rest with those who claim that capital punishment is an effective deterrent to capital crime. Let them build their castles in the air. For my own part, I have yet to see any real evidence that death deters more death. Speculation without hard evidence is just not acceptable, not when we are dealing with the ultimate sacredness of human life. The simple utterance of a statement does not make it fact. Are we to lower ourselves to the levels of the men and women we prosecute?

Let the retentionists prove that states which impose capital punishment have a substantially lower rate of murder than those which have abolished it. Since most available data shows this is simply not the case, why have proponents not conducted their own studies? Why have they not produced hard evidence to show that a highly publicized execution actually decreases the rate of murder by any appreciable amount? Proponents of capital punishment cannot point to a single neighborhood where this has happened. Surely "professional researchers" can locate at least one example. Let them convince me, with graphs and charts and mounds of statistics, that those states which have imposed the death penalty are now significantly freer from serious crime than prior to reinstitution. Again, there is not a single such correlation known. Let them poll the inhabitants of those states which use the death penalty, and find out if they feel safer on their streets than the citizens of the states which have repealed it. This is also apparently not the case. Florida, Texas, and California have thirty-two percent (696 of 1874) of the total number of inmates in the United States on death row.

The residents of capital punishment states are, in fact, *not* any safer than those in non-capital punishment states such as Michigan, Massachusetts, and New York. The murder rate per 100,000 for the year 1985 in Texas was 13.0; in Florida 11.4; in California 10.5. Their executions did not allow them to reduce murder per 100,000 below that of the non-capital punishment states of Michigan with 11.2; Massachusetts with 3.5, and New York with 9.5. Condemning to death the mass murderers of California, the drug kingpins of Florida, or the cowboy killers of Texas has not made Sunset Boulevard (in Los Angeles), Flagler Street (in Miami), or Main Street (in Houston) any safer than Broadway Street (in New York City).

Clearly, if the death penalty were the deterrent to major crime that its proponents claim, those states applying it least should show a much greater incidence of capital offenses. At the least, proponents should be able to demonstrate some direct relationship between the threat of capital punishment and the failure of criminals to engage in the sort of crimes to which capital punishment is applied. There is no such known correlation.

Advocates of the death penalty state that, without it, no adequate punishment is available to those already in prison who kill others after being incarcerated (including prison guards). Although the number of prison guards killed in the line of duty is small, even one constitutes grave concern for all those who respect the right to life and the rule of law, and there is no easy answer to this problem.

Organizations representing police officers have advocated imposition of the death penalty for premeditated murder, murder committed during felony crimes, and the killing of law enforcement and correctional officials while in the performance of duty. My friend and colleague, Representative Mario Biaggi of New York, a former police officer in New York City who was highly decorated for his bravery in the line of duty, introduced House Bill 2392 in 1987, an act which would do precisely what these organizations have requested.

Congressman Biaggi's legislation would allow states three years to adopt a death penalty statute for willfully killing a law enforcement officer, or that state would lose its share of federal criminal justice assistance, which currently totals approximately $350 million per year nationwide.

The arguments of the police associations for enacting such legislation in the twelve abolitionist states lose much of their vitality when measured against the arbitrary application of the death penalty in the thirty-eight states now using capital punishment (in each of these jurisdictions, the murder of a police officer is already punishable by death). In the state of Georgia, for instance, sixteen men have been arrested since 1972 for murdering police officers in Fulton County. Only one of these, Warren McCleskey, has actually been sentenced to death, the rest having received lesser sentences.

Similarly, the supposed concern on the part of many capital-punishment supporters for the lives of prison guards is somewhat suspect, given their reaction to the tragic events at Attica State Prison in the late 1960s. Their silence was eloquent when Nelson Rockefeller, then governor of New York, effectively ordered the mass slaughter of Attica prison guards to quell a rebellion of the prisoners. There was little public outcry against the strategy employed by the governor and its disastrous consequences. On the contrary, far too many citizens jubilantly praised Rockefeller when the storming of the prison resulted in the massacre of eleven guards and thirty-two inmates. Apparently, the lives of eleven faceless, nameless guards (not to mention the inmates, some of whom were guilty in this particular instance only of being in the wrong place at the wrong time) were not as important as the overwhelming need to restore order within the prison walls. Spiro T. Agnew, then vice president of the United States (he was later to resign his office under a cloud, due to previous felonious misconduct as the governor of Maryland), was one of the few American leaders who commented on the issue. Agnew spoke for his fellow supporters of capital punishment when he said:

> To position the "demands" of convicted felons in a place of equal dignity with legitimate aspirations of law-abiding American citizens—or to compare the loss of life by those whose job it is to uphold it—represents not simply an assault on human sensibility, but an insult to reason....The need to use force to break the strike does not lie in "social injustice"....[34]

Of course, the situation was volatile, the inmates were desperate, and they had already killed other guards and other inmates. And the guards knew the risks when they took the jobs. But it's also true that the order to kill them was an outrageous act, demonstrating reckless disregard for the lives of both guards and prisoners alike.

The fiasco at Attica raises fundamental questions about *who has the right to impose the death sentence.* In this case, the governor of New York assumed that prerogative, and actually ordered the deaths of inmates who were confined (even while rioting) in a restricted area without possibility of escape. In the process, innocent prison guards were subjected to the same sentence. Why supporters of the death penalty continue to glorify official violence while condemning random violence elsewhere is beyond all logic or reason.

If premeditated murder were the sole crime which could be punished by death, some of the argument for abolition would be silenced. All studies indicate that passion and provocation are the root causes of most violent crime against persons in the United States. It is a rare for murderers actually to plan the killing of a victim. A statistical report issued by the FBI in 1979 reveals that almost forty-three percent of murders committed in the U.S. involve some type of argument. Robbery and narcotics provided the motivations behind an additional twenty-seven percent.

If 5,642 "preplanned" murders took place in 1979, and less than 2,000 persons over the last ten years have been sentenced to death (and many fewer actually executed), it is easy to see that capital punishment is hardly applied in a uniform way. The vast majority of even those who commit premeditated murder escape the ultimate penalty. The gap is too wide to support the logic of those who argue that the death penalty applied in this manner serves as a deterrent.

Those who claim capital punishment serves as an effective deterrent against violent crime have failed to advance much beyond conjecture. They cannot substantiate even the most basic elements of their argument. Firstly, they must show that potential criminals pause, think, and make judgments about the consequences of being caught before they commit capital crimes. Secondly, the evidence must demonstrate that a person weighs the possibility of death or some lesser sentence before committing such an act. Thirdly, proponents must clearly prove that such considerations will, in a majority of cases, prevent the commission of murder. But the facts suggest otherwise. Most of the *hard* evidence available clearly indicates that potential murderers give little (if any) thought to being apprehended, and none at all to possible punishment. Many believe themselves "untouchable" by the law (or at least above the law), and usually find themselves in a state of total disbelief when the prosecution demands the death penalty. It has simply never occurred to them that capital punishment might be applied to *them*.

European studies of crime also demonstrate the failure of capital punishment as an effective deterrent. Robert Badinter, Minister of Justice of the French Republic, in a 1983 speech before Amnesty International, stated:

In this regard I would like to mention the French data, which are particularly precise and striking. Historically, as I mentioned during the abolition debate before the French Parliament, France is the only country in which there has been experimental evidence showing that abolition has no effect on deterrence.

Specifically, from 1888 to 1897, the various presidents of France made only sparing use of their powers of commutation, and the guillotine was in steady operation. The number of murders during that ten-year-period was 3,066. On the other hand, from 1898 to 1907, the presidents of France, who happened to be abolitionists, systematically commuted all death sentences. If the proponents of the death penalty as a means of deterrence are to be believed, this period of announced clemency should have brought about a striking increase in violent crime. What in fact happened? Exactly the opposite; while the guillotine was idle, the number of murders fell by fifty percent.[35]

Clearly, factors other than capital punishment were at work here. In the United States, the majority of those executed are petty criminals, both economically deprived and uneducated, with no economic or social prospects. The majority of those who evade execution are social *prima donnas*, highly educated and financially well-to-do, with the means and education to fight the law to a standstill. It seems reasonable to infer that the death penalty can have no pronounced deterrent affect on a class of people who cannot read, who often live life on an animalistic, dog-eat-dog level, and who neither appreciate nor value the sanctimony of human life, including their own. Likewise, death is no deterrent to a white-collar class which understands how the legal system might be circumvented. Even the Mafia dons recently convicted in New York, for all their heinous crimes, will never face death except at the hands of their brothers in the mob. They know it—*and we know it.*

These professional, hardened criminals, the most logical candidates who should have been deterred from their horrendous crimes, have as a class largely escaped the ultimate punishment. None of them has actually walked the last mile, or had to choose a last supper, in decades. In fact, not one person from the top hierarchy of a criminal syndicate, with the possible exception of Louis "Lepke" Buchalter, allegedly head of the infamous Murder, Incorporated, has ever been executed by the state, although thousands have died at the hands of their rivals in the crime syndicate. Strange to say, "Lepke" also measured up to our prescription for legalized murder, since he too was a member of a minority group, the Jews.

Alleged crime bosses Al (Scarface) Capone (Chicago), Frank Costello (N.Y.), Charles (Lucky) Luciano (N.Y.), Anthony Anastasia, Jack (Legs) Diamond, and Benjamin (Bugsy) Siegel all met fates other than the dreaded gallows. So is it really convincing to tell a sixteen-year-old ghetto kid that if he imitates the lives of the Capones and Lucianos he will end up on death row? He is far more likely to find himself the victim of drug overdose or gang warfare.

Rather than acting as a deterrent, the death penalty has significantly contributed to the killing, violence, and mayhem that have become an accepted way of life (official and unofficial) in America. With each act of murder, each act of mayhem, each act of violence, this society has become a little less civilized.

Gary Wills, writing in a column about the execution of his friend, pointedly questioned the basis of the deterrence theory when he said:

> We kill one person to deter some unknown person, somewhere, from killing....We are not entirely sure where or when (if ever) that deterrent effect will occur. But we are sure we have killed the man in the chair....There is no way to counter death but with life— we can mourn those who are lost only by saving those who are left, by treasuring life, by literally "discrediting" the currency of death. Otherwise, the cycle is unbreakable—the displaced people displacing others, the hated hating, the victims victimizing, the friends of the killed killing, and death collecting its debt.[36]

Totally ignoring such pleas for compassion, reason, and justice, the masses refuse to take issue with a national policy that is psychologically in synch with their own distorted opinions of capital punishment. Elected officials find their moral strength in popular opinion, and so the cycle is reinforced and continues in self-perpetuated motion. Acts of retaliation and revenge simply spark more of the same from society's enemies, internal or external, continuing a cycle which is almost impossible to break. As society retaliates, the criminal escalates. Violence, both unofficial and official, grows at an uninhibited rate. *When, where, how* will it all end?

7. The Menace of Handguns

The most striking reason that ten times as many persons are victims of homicide in the United States than in all of Western European countries combined is the ready availability of handguns in this country.

Stephen S. Trott, Assistant U.S. Attorney General, has totally failed to recognize the inconsistency of Justice Department logic in supporting legal executions as a deterrent to crime while simultaneously opposing strict restrictions on the proliferation of cheap handguns. In his testimony before a House of Representatives hearing, he stated:

> I have talked to countless detectives over the years....I was curious as to why criminals did what they did, and I was especially interested in [the effect of] the death penalty, and frequently, very often, I was advised by the detectives that when they asked these kinds of people: "Why did you use a toy or an empty gun?," the answer came back, "Hey, we know about felony murder. We are willing to ride the beef on a 211 (a robbery in California), but we are not willing to get tangled up in the death penalty." These were situations where an awareness of the death penalty by robbers protected victims from these types of offenses.[37]

Mr. Trott's testimony typifies the kind of unscientific data used to sanction the use of capital punishment. Firstly (and unconsciously), he admits that handguns are the primary instruments used in many robbery murders. One obvious solution to the problem, limiting the availability of the weapons so commonly (and lethally) employed in robberies, is ignored by Trott because it does not conform to the ideology of his administration. The official policy of the Reagan and Bush administrations has been to support the availability of handguns on demand. Secondly, if the threat of capital punishment has caused so many robbers to pause and consider the consequences, why has it not worked equally effectively with the many others who *do* commit armed robbery and kill their victims in the process? If such a threat had actually been effective, the state of California would not currently have more inmates than any other state awaiting execution for this exact same crime.

In the year 1980, only seventy-seven people were killed in Japan by handguns, eighteen in Sweden, eight in Great Britain, twenty-three in Israel, twenty-four in Switzerland, four in Australia, and eight in Canada. The total civilian population murdered by handguns in these seven civilized countries totalled just 278 out of 250 million. During the same year in the United States, a nation of equal population, 11,522 persons were killed by handguns.

The exorbitant number of murders in the United States does not necessarily indicate that the citizens of these other countries are somehow more civilized than we—I just don't believe that. It does mean, however, that such nations more scrupulously control the weapons of violence that are used to slaughter innocent people, and thereby have fewer random deaths caused by easy access to "Saturday Night specials."

Other advanced societies consider it a serious offense to possess handguns which serve no useful purpose except to kill other human beings. In our culture, the handgun is somehow viewed as a badge of honor, an idea left over from the frontier society of the Old West. No patriotic, red-blooded American would be caught without a Magnum .45 or a .38 special on his premises. The primary issue here is not our "right to bear arms," guaranteed under the Constitution, but our imagined need to do so. There is no Constitutional "right" to own a handgun—or flamethrower, bazooka, or any other proscribed weapon. The ready availability of millions of handguns has reduced the United States to an armed camp of citizen combatants where the murder rate looms ever larger and more uncontrollable.

Arguments used by those who oppose handgun control is naive at best, and catastrophic at worse. "Guns don't kill people—people kill people," trumpets the National Rifle Association. Such trite expressions do not begin to answer the basic question of why less than three hundred people were killed in one year by handguns in seven other civilized nations approximating the population of the United States, while over eleven thousand individuals were murdered with these same weapons here. We murder as many people in one month with handguns as the rest of the western world does in one year.

The "right to bear arms" is the most slanderously misinterpreted section of the Constitution. What that document actually states is "That a well-regulated militia being necessary to the security of a free state, the right of the people to keep and bear arms, shall not be infringed." This amendment was ratified when a citizen army was the only viable protection for this country, and a citizen's gun the only means of repelling wild (and human) animals on the American frontier. The national militia now has the responsibility of protecting this nation and its freedoms. The U.S. government and its fifty states are now spending billions of dollars a year to perform that task. In addition, the phrase "right to bear arms" is both vague and misleading. If the government can enact laws which make it illegal to possess machine guns and similar weapons without infringing on the constitutional rights of citizens, can it not impose the same conditions on other weapons which were not readily available at the time when the amendment was originally ratified? The Constitution must always be interpreted with a modicum of common sense.

If the abolition or reduction of murder in this country is the primary rationale for imposing the death penalty, and if handguns are the principle source of those murders (as they are), then simple logic dictates that handguns must be restricted to those individuals, such as law enforcement officers, who have a legitimate reason to carry them. Such restriction would not affect the use of rifles for hunting or other sporting purposes.

Unfortunately, organizations such as the National Rifle Association raise millions of dollars annually to propagandize the public into believing that the foundation of our democracy rests on the inalienable right of citizens to own pistols. Meaningless slogans are employed to panic the population to donate millions of dollars to the coffers of the NRA, and to lobby their elected officials to vote against gun control.

Legitimate arguments and real issues are brushed aside in a storm of emotional protests which precludes any real discussion about the control of handguns. Despite the fact that public opinion surveys show overwhelming support among the voters for control, the U.S. Congress refuses to enact legislation to achieve that end. A 1981 national survey conducted by Peter Hart indicates that 76% of American voters support handgun registration; 89% favor a waiting period between purchase and pickup of a handgun so that a police background check can be carried out; 77% favor banning small, cheap, low-quality handguns; 93% support mandatory sentences for the use of a handgun to commit a crime; 95% of voters surveyed support the requirement of a prompt reporting of the theft or loss of a handgun.

National polls have consistently revealed attitudes similar to those reported by pollster Hart. Yet, legislators at both the state and national level refuse to enact laws in this area. These very same legislators proudly cite polls indicating a majority of the public is opposed to abortions and favor the death penalty, but immediately ignore polls which fail to buttress their own opinions.

Those opposed to handgun control accept only those sections of such surveys that deal with the imposition of mandatory sentences for crimes committed by handguns. I also support this, as I do any legitimate effort to reduce crime in our cities (I represent a city district myself). But until the number of readily available guns in our communities is sharply reduced, mandatory sentencing for using them will not lessen the number of murders. The only result will be the massive overcrowding of jails that we are now seeing.

For the purpose of restrictive legislation, a "handgun" is described as a pistol or revolver, easily concealable, not to be confused with such hunting weapons as rifles and shotguns. Pistols and revolvers are the primary instruments of violent crimes; in 1982 the United States experienced 9,055 deaths attributable to handguns, plus 145,610 aggravated assaults, and 214,755 robberies in which handguns played a part. If the fifty or sixty million handguns now in the homes of American citizens were not in their possession, no other weapon capable of causing such misery and suffering would be available as a replacement. Banning the manufacture, sale, and transfer of handguns is critical to any effort to reduce violent crime in this country. If handguns kill people, and if many people use handguns to kill other people, then many people would not be killed if their friends, neighbors, family, or local criminals did not have easy access to such weapons. Handgun control is a logical, reasonable, first step in a realistic program of deterrence.

V.

WHY NOT PUBLIC EXECUTIONS?

Anybody whose pleasure is watching somebody else die is about as little use to humanity as the person being electrocuted.

—Will Rogers

1. THE SECRECY OF DEATH

As long as the names of the victims are kept in a secret dossier, as long as the ritual is conducted for private consumption, witnessed exclusively by a privileged few, carried out behind closed doors, capital punishment can have no measurable deterrent value on the public at large. The act of taking faceless victims, harbored in isolated dungeons, walking through long corridors to lonely death chambers, is so prescribed as not to disturb the serenity of law-abiding citizens. The theory of deterrence cannot influence a general public that is unaware an execution has taken place, the reasons for it, or the torturousness of the death itself.

If capital punishment is to serve as a deterrent, this country must emulate the example set by China. There executions are in public and carried out by a single shot in the back of the head. According to Wang Jingrong, a spokesman for China's Ministry of Public Security, public executions have had a definite impact on criminal activity. During the year 1983, an estimated 5,000 to 10,000 people were executed in China for crimes such as pimping, armed robbery, spying, embezzling and organizing secret societies. Wang said, "The facts show that the executions of a small number of criminals guilty of the most heinous crimes have contributed to the education of the majority of the criminals. The crime rate has dropped from a high of eight offenses per 10,000 persons to a current rate of five offenses per 10,000."[1]

95

Laws in the U.S. differ substantially from state to state in determining how and when executions may be witnessed, and by what specific numbers and types of individuals. Arizona's criminal code mandates that the prison superintendent be present at all executions, and instructs him to invite a physician, the state attorney general, and at least twelve reputable citizens. The defendant has a right to invite two clergymen, relatives, or friends, not to exceed five additional persons. Oklahoma statutes are identical to those of Arizona, with one exception: reporters from recognized newspapers, press and wire services, or radio and TV stations are permitted with the advance approval of the warden. In Utah, the only person compelled to attend is a physician named by the warden. The warden himself is not required to be present. California is similar to the others, except the law specifically prohibits attendance by any person under legal age. Missouri also prohibits the witness of an execution by any person under the age of twenty-one years. Louisiana restricts anyone under the age of eighteen.

Ironically, all three states *authorize executions of persons under the age of eighteen.* Perhaps, in their opinion, there is something morbid about the idea of one youth seeing the life of another snuffed out by the legal agents of the government.

The state of North Carolina relieves the warden of any personal responsibility in the process of administering the lethal gas to the victims, specifically mandating him to designate a guard or other reliable person to perform the actual execution. Further, it limits the expenditures of the prison's board of directors for such purposes to thirty-five dollars. This measure is false economy in any language. In fact, it costs on the average of more than $1 million in taxpayers' monies to successfully get one criminal to the point of actually being executed. Louisiana law mandates that all executions must take place between midnight and 3 A.M. No one seems to remember why.

Alabama and Ohio laws contain another novel twist, forbidding other convicts from witnessing the execution of one of their fellows. If the purpose of capital punishment is to deter others from committing murder, and if the jails of every state are filled with potential candidates for murdering others, one would think that attendence by every prison inmate should be made compulsory. What better way to warn them of the potentially serious side effects of their criminous activity!

Carried to its logical extremes (if one employs the distorted logic of those supporting capital punishment), to have the maximum possible effect in deterring crime, executions should be publicly displayed and exhibited, as they were in previous centuries. If supporters of capital punishment are serious about the deterrent value of the ultimate penalty, they would support public executions as a meaningful vehicle for informing the greatest number of potential criminals that crime really does not pay. After all, that was the method of capital punishment during the early years of this nation. Executions in the thirteen colonies were public for the first 150 years of American history, and some states continued this practice until the beginning of the 20th century. Why proponents of capital punishment should oppose such public displays is both self-contradictory and hypocritical, and certainly has more to do with a fear of public reactions (and the resulting political consequences) than with any real theory of penology. In other words, reinstitution of public executions might lead ordinary people to begin agitating for abolition of the death penalty.

In March of 1984, James David "Cowboy" Autry requested that his injection with Sodium Pentothal be televised nationally. Texas Attorney General Jim Mattox, supporting the prisoner's plea, said that if executions are to serve as a deterrent, they must be done in public. But a federal judge denied the request that TV cameras be permitted in the death chamber. The Texas Board of Corrections voted 8-0 to ban such broadcasts, because, they said (speaking through their Chairman, Robert Gunn), public executions would "just [be] in bad taste." How perceptive! How perspicacious! How perverse! Yes, Mr. Gunn, executions, whether public or private, are indeed the ultimate in bad taste. Deliberately taking the life of a human being cannot be elevated to some sanctimonious plateau by command of any government.

"Cowboy" Autry served the public interest in demanding a public execution. Those who opposed it did not. Their rationales prove most interesting. Billy Hughes, another death row inmate, accused Texas officials of trying to disguise their own premeditated murder of convicts. Opponents of capital punishment challenged the Corrections Board to televise the execution. Public officials, including the governors who have routinely refused to commute such sentences, and the conservative-leaning newspaper editors who have crowed over each state-sponsored death (as if *any* death, of *any* man, was something to celebrate), suddenly fell silent on this most pressing question. This is not unusual. Every politician loves an execution—so long as it is kept safely out of public eyes. The less public the overt cruelties of capital punishment, the less chance of any serious debate about its implementation.

However, there is no realistic foundation for assuming that public executions would necessarily cause the demise of capital punishment—or, for that matter, deter others from engaging in capital crimes. As Albert Camus noted in a 1957 essay:

Even if executions were on television, there is no guarantee that prospective ax murderers would pay heed. When pickpockets were punished by hanging in England, other thieves exercised their talents in the crowds surrounding the scaffold where their fellow was being hanged.[2]

Today, public executions in such countries as China, Saudi Arabia, Lebanon, and Kenya are commonly thought to deter further crime—based on theories of penology that were current in ancient times. But throughout the centuries, most civilized nations have eventually come to realize that official violence is counterproductive, that the lust for blood—or revenge—is rooted in basic animalistic needs. Self-protection does not normally require such measures as capital punishment. As Ellen Goodman wrote in a UPI wire story:

It's been almost 50 years since the public could watch an execution in the United States. One of the last public hangings occurred at dawn, August 26, 1936, when a man named Raine Bethea was hung before a raucus crowd of 10,000 in Owensboro, Kentucky. We are told, in a vivid account by *Time* magazine, that the spectators had spent the night before Bethea's death drinking and attending hanging parties. Through the early hours of that day, hawkers squeezed their way through the crowd selling popcorn and hot dogs. Telephone poles and trees were festooned with spectators.

By 5 o'clock, the crowd grew impatient, began to yip, "Let's bring him out." At 5:20 a.m., Bethea, his stomach bulging with chicken, pork chops and watermelon, was pushed through the crowd to the base of the platform. At 5:28 there was a swish, a snap. Soon the spectators crowded in and "eager hands clawed at the black death hood...the lucky ones stuffed the bits of black cloth in their pockets."[3]

What a grotesque, gruesome reaction from a supposedly civilized community! Still, if we must have executions, they *should* be public displays, if they are to serve any public purpose. In modern America, however, secrecy is the polite, gentlemanly way of disposing of our societal garbage.

France and England engaged in this degenerate type of activity for centuries, only to learn it engendered a spirit of incivility amongst the populace. Subsequently, both countries abolished the death penalty because it failed to deter serious crime, and because it was repulsive to the human spirit. They found public executions so dehumanizing that society was the loser in the final analysis.

So repugnant is the practice of capital punishment that both the victim and the public are adversely affected by this tortuous, wholly unreasonable method for disposing of criminals. It is not for the benefit of the hanged that some states require blindfolds to be placed over their heads, but for the emotional relief of the hangman. He (or *she*—should not death be an equal opportunity employer?) is spared the vulgar necessity of looking his helpless victim straight in the eye, of witnessing another human who has done nothing personally to him die at his hands. Similarly, while state firing squads may be composed of expert marksmen, one or more of them are always issued dummy ammunition. The condemned man is placed on a chair with a big "X" marked on his chest and a screen obscuring his face. The knowledge that blank bullets fill the magazines of at least some of the rifles supposedly absolves any specific individual from guilt. Why do we go through these charades? Why is the warden who pulls the switch on the electric chair always in another room, out of sight of the executed? Is this deterrence? Is this fair? Is this open? Who are we hiding from? In most states the identity of official executioners must be kept hidden from the public. Why?

> Most states take precautions to protect his (the executioner's) identity. Florida, for example, garbs him in a medieval black cloak and hood. Other states sometimes diffuse responsibility so even the participants need not take the blame: three guards press buttons to activate the electric chair, but two buttons are dummies. In Utah, one of the rifles fired at Gary Gilmore contained a blank bullet, and each member of the firing squad believes that his weapon had fired it.[4]

The impact of capital punishment on individuals participating in the process has been very movingly and effectively described in a recent book, *Deathman Pass Me By*, by Philip Brasfield, a prisoner at the Tennessee Colony of the Texas State Prison System, as told to Dr. Jeffrey M. Elliot, Professor of Political Science, North Carolina Central University, Durham, North Carolina. Mr. Brasfield is presently awaiting retrial after being convicted and sentenced to death, and then agonizing on death row for two years before the Court of Appeals overturned his conviction. He writes:

> After I heard the pronouncement, I looked up at the jury box. Not one person would meet my glance. Each head was bowed as if in meditation; their eyes could have bored holes into the floor. All I heard was Judge William Shaver shuffling some papers; someone behind me scraped a chair on his way out. The burly deputies who were assigned as guards motioned me through the side door, where I joined my ashen-faced mother and my wife, who was in tears.[5]

Even the new, supposedly "humane" types of execution have not been able to reconcile the irreconcilable dilemma between man's insatiable desire to cling to his own life and his readiness to snuff out that of his brother. In the end, someone must still pull the trigger/press the switch/release the drop/*kill the prisoner*, and however much we try to sanitize the process, one man still dies and another is brutalized, and the the society which supports the process inevitably made harsher, less kind, less gentle, less civilized. Our thousand points of light are rapidly becoming a thousand funeral pyres blazing in the night of this new dark age.

If the death penalty is to act as a deterrent, all segments of society must be able to view the process, so that the object lesson is lost on none. Should there not be mandatory attendance by school children, who might someday be tempted to commit such heinous crimes? Or perhaps proponents would limit such attendance to black and brown and yellow children, or just those from poor families.

We can see the harsh effects of capital punishment mirrored on the faces of those actually involved in the process—family, friends, jurors, jurists, police, and prison officials—frozen in a rictus of pain, sorrow, and savagery. Once again, the account of Philip Brasfield (who was there) is most instructive:

> Josie [his wife], Ma, and I waited a little more than thirty minutes before I was called back into the court-

room where the judge would sentence me to die by lethal injection, but first he thanked the jury and dismissed them, saving them from watching me stand and hear the outcome of their deliberations. Not one looked at me. I searched their faces and saw only stone masks. Yet, I wondered if they were able to go home and pretend that they had not, somehow, changed. I wondered how, after sealing my fate, they could grasp the fabric of everyday life they had briefly dropped, and not find it torn and shredded.[6]

Brasfield's brutal picture of a Wichita County, Texas court house is reinforced by South Carolina trial lawyer David Bruck, an expert witness on capital punishment. Speaking before the U.S. House of Representatives Subcommittee on Criminal Justice, he stated:

I don't think the environment is quite what we would imagine from looking at the Gallup polls. I think in reality the American people and the people in South Carolina have a great ambivalence about the death penalty. And that, more than any legal appeals or legal technicalities, is the reason why we have condemned so many but executed so few. I think the American people at a deep level of our consciousness have already abolished the death penalty and don't know it. In other words, we have seen to a large extent morally and emotionally the same developments that have occurred in every other democracy...which has already abolished capital punishment.[7]

These examples are precisely the reasons some states are replacing the gas chamber with lethal injections. Killing even a convicted murderer is too painful and too barbaric for decent people to witness. Ingenious men who support capital punishment are constantly looking for new ways to render this torturous episode more humane, and thus more compatible to modern American sensitivities.

Injections are usually associated with medical and therapeutic efforts to heal the body, not to destroy it. Adolf Hitler used similar methods (now widely condemned) for the purpose of human experimentation. His stated reasons were lofty indeed, to improve medical science and prolong life. Pumping doses of sodium thiopental into one's arm has only one purpose, stated or otherwise—to terminate a human life.

Every instrument officially employed by states to take the life of human beings contradicts in some way the purpose for which that instrument was originally patented. Gunpowder was developed by a German monk, Berthold Schwarz, who actually envisioned it as a means of deterring war. His theory was similar to the one now held by many military and political theorists in our world: the proliferation of nuclear weapons combined with the frightening consequences of unleashing them will actually deter their use and actually prevent wars. Today, gunpowder is one of the prescribed methods of execution in the United States. Electricity and gas were initially exploited to lessen the burdens of humanity. Today, they are also the most preferred methods of snuffing out the lives of those convicted of crimes. Jacob used a rope to construct a ladder to climb to heaven, not to hang infidels.

With a little imagination and very little ingenuity, executions could be used by our financially-strapped state and federal governments to generate much-needed revenues. Now that lottery fever has fallen off in those states which have introduced institutionalized gambling, why not introduce weekly television programs bringing *real* death to prime-time TV? These would be supported, of course, by the appropriate commercial enterprises and groups benefitting from legal executions. Soon major sponsors would be jumping at the chance to start game shows in which the contestants would decide what bizarre forms of death were appropriate for this week's criminal. We could even have "Barabbas" shows in which one or more crooks were pardoned (as the result of each contestant's success or failure), the rest being summarily executed at the program's climax. And not only would these new sources of revenue revitalize the public coffers, but (as in ancient Rome) the blood lust of the public would be satisfied.

Published statistics do not bear out the fact that public or private executions increase or decrease the rate of first-degree murders. But if there is to be any real deterrent value, executions of all homicidal maniacs must become common, well-publicized occurrences. Of course, this will not happen in modern America. Too many politicians who support capital punishment also believe that extensive exposure of the process would prompt a massive campaign by the public to outlaw all executions. They remember that live television coverage of Americans dropping napalm bombs on old men, middle-aged women, and innocent young children helped end the war in Vietnam. Similarly, live TV coverage showing hundreds or thousands of real-life executions would spur public opinion to hasten the prohibition of state-sponsored killings. The twisted, turning limbs, charred flesh, and facial grimaces of excruciating pain would cause the most hardened individuals to collectively regurgitate.

In order to achieve maximum deterrent value (if this is what they are meant to achieve), public executions must be shown and promoted on a large-scale basis. To further enhance their commercial value, the government should employ slick public relations gimmicks, extensive advertising, quality media productions, and sensational dramatizations. Obviously, something more exciting than just a drab hanging or a dull lethal injection would be required.

Singing the national anthem, raising the flag, beating the drums, and, of course, inviting fundamentalist preachers to provide selective readings from the Old Testament would add immeasurably to the occasion. Popcorn for children, beer for adults, pom-pom girls, and score cards would be prerequisites for such extravaganzas. The president of the United States could call the jury foreman, the governor, and the executioner to offer his congratulations. Any aspirant for high public office would be sitting idly on the sidelines, waiting to offer his kudos and to kiss any babies who might be present.

Public executions, in order to deter crime, should be turned into the equivalent of the Super Bowl or World Series. Las Vegas bookmakers could then lay odds on how fast the criminals would die, how long each of them would twitch. Perhaps the state lotteries could get into the act.

If all of this sounds grotesque, well of course it is—the murder of any human being, however despicable personally, is not a pleasant experience. Such public displays will generate one of two responses: either overwhelming citizen acceptance or outright rejection. There can be no middle ground. This is a moral question, which, if presented to two hundred and fifty million Americans in a forthright way, must result in some firm decision. Unfortunately, no one can accurately predict now what the answer might be, although I personally believe that no sane, moral individual could condone such violence if he was able to view the consequences.

The primary reason politicians have insisted on private executions is obvious: they do not really believe in the deterrence value of capital punishment, but they are willing to cater to the avowed public desire for official revenge. Only occasionally in recent decades have elected officials in a position to affect the outcome of death sentences taken a strong public stand against state-sponsored executions. In fact, only two governors in our history have vacated death rows by commuting the sentences of all death-row inmates to life in prison. Governor Winthrop Rockefeller of Arkansas did it in 1970, and Governor Toney Anaya of New Mexico, just prior to retiring in 1986, commuted the sentences of five men awaiting execution to life in prison. Commenting on the situation, Rockefeller said: "For me to simply walk away now will make me as much an accomplice as others who would participate in their executions."[8] Anaya made similar comments thirty-three days before leaving office. The incoming governor, Garrey Carruthers, a Republican and supporter of capital punishment, had campaigned against leniency for convicted felons. During an election in which Governor Anaya was prohibited by state law from seeking another term, Carruthers said, "The first thing I want to see on my desk after I'm elected Governor is the paperwork necessary to restart the death penalty."[9] Governor Anaya, who came under much pressure from conservative groups in New Mexico for his actions, stated:

> Capital punishment is a false god that all too many worship....Capital punishment is inhumane, immoral, anti-God and incompatible to an enlightened society....It is my prayer that New Mexico can become the birthplace of an idea whose time has come—the elimination of the death penalty once and for all and the establishment of, and commitment to, a moral, just and effective criminal justice system in its place.[10]

If supporters of capital punishment are serious about the deterrence value of the maximum penalty, then they will openly support public executions as the best means of deterring the maximum number of potentially violent people. To do otherwise admits serious doubt about their basic philosophical position.

The same public opinion polls which reveal that the majority of Americans support capital punishment also indicate they were appalled, shocked, and incensed as they watched on national television a South Vietnamese colonel place his pistol to the head of an alleged Viet Cong supporter and blow his brains out. Some will argue that this incident was out of the ordinary, and certainly cannot be condoned as an acceptable method of execution in a civilized society. But it is the same method used today on mainland China. Even petty criminals are executed by firing a bullet in the back of the head while the offender kneels. On September 21, 1989, in the city of Jeddah, the Saudi Arabian government beheaded in public sixteen Kuwaiti nationals (Moslem Shiites) who were convicted of bombing the Mosque during the Holy Pilgrimage season.

Brains and eggs are a favorite breakfast food in some parts of our

To Kill or Not to Kill

country. But splattered brains coming across the television at dinner time might be biting off more than America can eat. The episode of the Vietnamese colonel has convinced many that public executions would be the beginning of the end of *all* executions. In my opinon, the new generation of Americans accustomed to easy suburban living, who claim to abhor pornography, sex education, and abortion, simply will not tolerate such public obscenities. As an example, I offer the following fictional episode for the edification of future television viewers everywhere:

THE EXECUTION OF GERI WELFALL

Good evening. I'm John Smith of XYZ Television, speaking to you from our Cleveland Studios, bringing you the latest on today's stellar event. This afternoon, blond, blue-eyed, Geri Welfall, a white female, age 16, 5 feet 1 inch tall, and weighing 98 pounds, became the 610th person to be executed in the United States this year. Little Geri was convicted on September 2, 1992, in Cleveland Superior Court of armed robbery and first degree murder. The **ALL-MALE, ALL-BLACK** jury found her guilty of luring the victim, Willie Bobo, a 260-pound Black construction worker, into a deserted, wooded area, robbing him of his week's salary, and crushing his head with a baseball bat.

The pathologist testified in court that he found numerous abrasions over the entire body of Mr. Bobo, with extensive amounts of blood coming from the nose and mouth areas. There were three severe wounds found in the head area. The skull was fractured and multiple abrasions were found on the victim's arms, legs, and chest.

The Ohio State Supreme Court denied Geri's appeal by a 7-2 vote. Judge Hangum, writing for the majority, stated, "In a colorblind society, the mere coincidence that Ms. Welfall was convicted by an ALL-MALE, ALL-BLACK jury in a city seventy percent WHITE and sixty-percent FEMALE does not in and of itself constitute sexual, class, or racial bias." We must agree. Judge Hangum further stated: "The mere fact that the last 75 persons executed in Cleveland have been white, middle-class women, does not in and of itself prove any kind of racial, sexual, or class discrimination, as today's Conservation Coalition (Co-Co) has claimed. When all the factors—and the crime itself—have been properly accounted for, there can be no significant disparity between Blacks and whites, male and female, rich and poor, in the dispensing of justice."

He further stated that eighty-one preemptory strikes by the prosecution from a potential jury panel of eighty-one white females did not demonstrate sexually- or racially-motivated actions against Ms Welfall. The opinion enumerated the circumstantial nature of most of the evidence presented to the court, including failure of the prosecutor to sufficiently rebut fifteen eye witnesses, one a Catholic priest, who all testified that Geri was being baptized at the time of the murder. Casts of footprints taken at the murder scene, indicating the killer wore a size 12A shoe, and probably weighed between 190 and 210 pounds, were dismissed by the court as "speculative defense dramatization." Fingerprints found on the murder weapon at the scene, matching those of another suspect, J. H. Dillinger, were described by the prosecutor as "immaterial and irrelevant."

We will return after a short break to hear from our sponsors, said Mr. Smith.

Now, stated the anchorman, we switch to Roger Dirt, our field reporter who is at the scene of the execution, Sing Song Prison in Ohio. Roger will describe the events that took place earlier today as we run our video tape.

Thank you, John. It's always a pleasure to assist America's efforts to make our streets safe. Now, let's all see just how little Geri Welfall died.

You can see the executioner securing the noose around Geri's scrawny neck. Note that the knot is just under her left ear—I'm told, John, this is a very humane form of execution, and you can see how careful everyone is to get the details just right. Warden Henry Goering has just given the nod to proceed. He's raising his hand, and the guard in the next room has seen it.

They've cut the springs which will set off the trap! Oh, will you look at that!—Little Geri has just hit the bottom, and you can see that she is fighting, pulling on the straps, wheezing, whistling, wrestling. Just like a fish on a string. Who would have thought she'd give it such a fight! She seems to be trying to get air, and blood is oozing through the black cap over her head. You may not be able to see it, but she has urinated and defecated, and the droppings are now falling to the floor. God, this is great!—I hope all of red-blooded male America is watching, to see what happens to the scum who prowl our city streets.

Well, her body is just dangling now like a wind-blown kite, her arms and legs limp. I think that's just about it, John.

We're switching now from the victim to the eye witnesses. Ha, a couple of them are just greenhorns, as you can see—three have collapsed and are being carried out of the room on stretchers. Two others are vomiting. Nervous ninnies is what we old hands call them; I think they ought to be candidates for the rope themselves. No problem with the minister, though—he's seen a hundred come and go. The teary-eyed fellow in the grey suit is Sam Jones of the *Cleveland Gazette*. He covered the story from start to finish, and always claimed that Geri was innocent. He seems to be in a state of complete shock. Personally, I think she got what she deserved, and I know most Americans feel exactly the same way. Notice how cool the doctor is: now there's a professional for you. He's casually placing a stool in front of Geri's lifeless frame, ripping open her blouse, placing the stethoscope to her still-warm breast. What a waste, eh! We don't have time to show you his conscientiousness, but he repeated his gesture six times during a thirteen-minute period before finally pronouncing her dead.

Let's get some eyewitness impressions: I have here Martha Mayflower. Ms. Mayflower, was this your first execution?

"Oh no, Roger, I've been to many others. It's just so great to see the wheels of justice actually put in motion. Now, all the potential Geris in the country will know that the right to life is sacred. What I liked most was when they took her down from the gallows. Did you see where the noose had cut into her neck? Her eyes had rolled back, her tongue was swollen, and her face had turned purple. It was great!"

Thank you, Martha...and what group do you represent?

"Well, Roger, I'm National President of the Sanctity of Life Organization. We're Pro-Life, you know. I've witnessed all of the 610 executions we've had this year, some in person, some on the tube, but this is the first time I've been interviewed. It's just so very exciting."

Ms. Mayflower, is there anything that you want to say about capital punishment?

"Oh yes, it's just so great that I think it should be mandatory for all murderers and rapists and abortionists. If we don't execute all of the criminals, people will start losing confidence in the criminal justice system."

You head one of the largest pro-life organizations in the country; Don't you find something just a wee bit contradictory in your position?

"Oh no, Roger, Geri Welfall's life was sacred until she lost the confidence of the Lord—then she became a menace to society."

This is Roger Dirt. And that's the way it is, Saturday, September 3, 1992, just twenty-four hours after Geri's conviction and appellate court denial, where we've just seen the latest application of America's "swift justice" system. Thank you all, and goodnight.

2. SWIFT JUSTICE?

Execution twenty-four hours after conviction may seem rather farfetched to those accustomed to endless appeals and other delays. But anything is possible once the "killing" mentality sets in. During the 1940s and 1950s there was no guaranteed right of appeal in capital crime cases. Consequently, executions were swiftly carried out. In one case involving the 1953 kidnap/murder of a young child, the state of Missouri executed a woman and man just eleven weeks after their joint convictions.

Another case in South Carolina was even swifter in proceeding from trial to execution. George Stinney, a fourteen-year-old boy weighing just 95 pounds, was executed six weeks after being convicted of beating two little white girls to death with a railroad spike.

If television coverage of a real hanging would be in bad taste, imagine what Hollywood could do with an execution by lethal gas. The following gruesome scenes are lifted verbatim from an actual court case, *Gray vs. Lucas*, concerning an appeal of a death sentence in the state of Mississippi. Contending that death by lethal gas was cruel and unusual punishment, Gray submitted affidavits from three persons who had witnessed executions by lethal gas.

Tad Dunbar, a television news anchorman, attended the 1979 Nevada execution of Jesse Walter Bishop by lethal gas. Dunbar attests that he was "shocked and horrified" that death came only after Bishop's protracted struggle with the lethal cyanide gas:

> When the cyanide gas reached him, he gasped, and convulsed strenuously. He stiffened. His head lurched back. His eyes widened, and he strained as much as the straps that held him to the chair would allow. He unquestionably appeared in pain.
>
> Periodically now, perhaps at thirty-second intervals, he would convulse, alternately straining and relaxing in the chair. I noticed he had urinated. The convulsions continued for approximately ten more minutes, and you could see his chest expand, and then contract, trying to take in fresh air. These movements became weaker as the minutes ticked away. You could not tell when Bishop finally lost consciousness.[11]

Jesse Walter Bishop died at 12:21 a.m., exactly twelve minutes after the cyanide pellets were deposited in the gas chamber. A part of American civilization died at 12:09 a.m., the moment the first pellet was dropped into that chamber.

Another newsperson, Howard Brodie of CBS, witnessed the 1967 execution in California of Aaron Mitchell. He described the tragic event as follows:

> The pellets of cyanide were released by mechanical controls, and dropped into an acid jar beneath the chair. The gas rose, and seemed to hit him immediately. Within the first minute Mitchell slumped down. I thought to myself how quickly cyanide really worked.
>
> Within 30 seconds he lifted his head upwards again. He raised his entire body, arching, tugging at his straps. Saliva was oozing from his mouth. His eyes open, he turned his head to the right. He gazed through my window. His fingers were tightly gripping his thumbs. His chest was visibly heaving in sickening agony. Then he tilted his head higher, and rolled his eyes upward. Then he slumped forward. Still his heart was beating. It continued for another several minutes.[12]

On this occasion, the victim was pronounced dead approximately twelve minutes later. When the lethal capsule was released, society lost a little more of its respectability.

The Reverend Myer Tobey, S.J., saw the execution of Eddie Daniels in a Maryland penitentiary during the late 1950s. Writing as if his pen had been touched by the artistic hands of Michelangelo, Father Tobey reflected:

> In an instant, puffs of light white smoke began to rise. Daniels saw the smoke, and moved his head to try to avoid breathing it in. As the gas continued to rise he moved his head this way and that way, thrashing as much as his straps would allow still in an attempt to avoid breathing. He was like an animal in a trap, with no escape, all the time being watched by his fellow humans in the windows that lined the chamber. He could steal only glimpses of me in his panic, but I continued to repeat "My Jesus I love you," and he too would try to mouth it.
>
> Then the convulsions began. His body strained as much as the straps would allow. He had inhaled the deadly gas, and it seemed as if every muscle in his body was straining in reaction. His eyes looked as if they were bulging, much as a choking man with a rope cutting off his windpipe. But he could get no air in the

chamber.

Then his head dropped forward. The doctor in the observation room said that that was it for Daniels. This was within the first few minutes after the pellets had dropped. His head was down for several seconds. Then, as we had thought it was over, he again lifted his head in another convulsion. His eyes were open, he strained and he looked at me. I said one more time, automatically, "My Jesus I love you." And he went with me, mouthing the prayer. **He was still alive after those several minutes, and I was horrified.** He was in great agony. Then he strained and began the words with me again. I knew he was conscious, this was not an automatic response of an unconscious man. But he did not finish. His head fell forward again.

There were several more convulsions after this, but his eyes were closed. I could not tell if he were conscious or not at that point. Then he stopped moving, approximately ten minutes after the gas began to rise, and was officially pronounced dead.[13]

Execution by lethally injected gas may be less painful than crucifixion and strangulation, but under no circumstances can it be defined as humane. As far as the electric chair is concerned, I cite recent Supreme Court testimony which demonstrates the vile, violent expedition of electrical currents through a human body:

...when the switch is thrown, the condemned prisoner cringes, leaps and fights the straps with amazing strength. The hands turn red, then white, and the cords of the neck stand out like steel bands. The prisoner's limbs, fingers, toes, and face are severely contorted. The prisoner's eyeballs sometimes pop out and rest on his cheeks. The prisoner often defecates, urinates, and vomits blood and drool.

The body turns bright red as its temperature rises...the flesh swells and his skin stretches to the point of breaking. Sometimes the prisoner catches on fire, particularly if he perspires excessively. Witnesses hear a loud and sustained sound like bacon frying, and the sickly sweet smell of burning flesh permeates the chamber. This smell of frying human flesh in the immediate neighborhood of the chair is some times bad enough to nauseate even the press representatives who are present. In the meantime, the prisoner almost literally boils: the temperature in the brain itself approaches the boiling point of water, and when the post-electrocution autopsy is performed the liver is so hot that doctors have said that it cannot be touched by the human hand. The body frequently is badly burned and disfigured.[14]

The more things change, the more they remain the same. Even though executions are now held deep within the private confines of dreary prison walls, observed by only the privileged few, recent executions have included scenes similar to those of the 1936 Owensboro, Kentucky hanging. In 1977, when Gary Mark Gilmore challenged the state of Utah to place him before a firing squad, the crowd outside the prison chanted and cheered. T-shirts with Gilmore's image were hawked by street vendors. In October, 1983, at Huntsville, Texas, while James D. Autry awaited his execution, a crowd of people outside sang and shouted and rejoiced, chanting over and over again the refrain, "Kill him, kill him."

In October of 1984, hundreds of college students cheered the death of Thomas Andy Barefoot at a Texas penitentary, shouting and waving mock lethal syringes. Unlike the students killed at Kent State University, who died demonstrating against a meaningless war which was destroying the lives of thousands, this new generation of scholars showed its distortion of real values in demonstrating their support for legalized murder. A month later, at Raleigh, North Carolina, Velma Barfield became the first woman executed in the United States since 1952. A small crowd of thirty to forty opponents of the death penalty gathered outside the walls, carrying lighted candles. Soon three hundred other demonstrators had arrived, displaying placards which read, "The law is the law." Some even advanced the argument that cyanide injection is cost-effective, comparing the $104.04 figure for using cyanide gas to the $30.12 price tag of lethal injection.

It was a long time in the making, but the execution of this white woman, Velma Barfield, signifies that the chickens are finally coming home to roost. Indiscriminate killings of Black people, either through legal executions or mob lynchings, diminishes the respect for the lives of all others. A society which adamantly refuses to speak out against such atrocities, only delays the day when the sanctity of life for other citizens, even white women, will be snuffed out in such a casual manner.

The Gilmores, Autrys, Barefoots, and Barfields are mere pawns in a great chess game called survival of the societal fittest. Most Americans know little about the circumstances of their lives or deaths—and most don't care. Most of those who do care enough to be indignant never express their concerns to anyone but close relatives or friends.

Public demonstrators for enforcement of the death penalty seem to forget (conveniently) that only the poorer classes endure its ravishing sting—or perhaps it is just easier to blame the impoverished, the Blacks, the Chicanos, or other minority groups, for society's ills. Many politicians support capital punishment because they perceive it as an easy method for demonstrating their support for the war against crime. Where we once had "hanging judges," we now have "hanging governors," as witnessed by the following interview with a fictional person who very well could be governor of at least thirty-seven of our states. While reading this make-believe scenario, pause and reflect on similar statements made by some of your local elected officials.

AN INTERVIEW WITH GOVERNOR WILL KILLUM

"We now take you to the state capitol, where Governor Will Killum is standing by for a live television interview. Governor, thirty-seven felons have been executed during your first term. Why the large increase?"

"As you know, John, most of the voters of this state favor capital punishment. I believe that I was elected to reflect the will of the people. It's not surprising, then, that my hard-line stand is popular, and that the same polls that track these attitudes also reveal strong support for my reelection."

"But isn't it true, Governor, that you were elected to serve the best interests of the citizens, and not just transient political themes or popular slogans...?"

"I do not base my decisions solely on the polls or other evidence of the popular will. I sincerely believe that those who willfully kill should receive the same punishment in return. Since many citizens of this state obviously share these views, I can only suppose that they elected the man whom they felt most closely mirrored their own ideas, on this and other issues."

"No one doubts your sincerity, sir. Of course, many have wondered why this state still has one of the highest murder rates of any in America, and why overall crime under your administration has risen significantly, according to the latest statistics published by the FBI."

"Mr. Smith, you in the media are always carping and complaining, always attempting to confuse the issue. We have a sick society here, and the average citizen is fed up with playing the victim. I am only responding to the frustrations of the people of this state. They feel better when a criminal is caught, tried, and executed. The great majority of people in this great state are law-abiding and clean-living, and can immediately see the devious motivation of your question. I don't answer to you or anyone else except the citizens who have elected me, and will (I hope) continue to do so for the foreseeable future."

"Governor, there seems to be some disparity in the way the death penalty is applied in this state. I speak, of course, of your recent commutation of the death sentence in the case of the wealthy industrialist, W. Ellsworth Sockefellow."

"Mr. Smith, let me speak frankly about that case. Mr. Sockefellow has broken the law, and of course he must pay, just like any other citizen. He bludgeoned his wife and four kids to death with a sledge hammer. But up to this point, Sockefellow had been a model member of the community, a hardworking businessman with deep roots in this state. How do I balance this man's solid contributions to society with some common criminal's consistent record of transgressions dating back ten or fifteen or twenty years? There's just no comparison. That's why I set aside the jury verdict and placed him on parole."

"Is there any truth to the rumors, Governor, that Mr. Sockefellow was a heavy contributor to your last campaign?"

"Mr. Smith, I don't know who contributed to my last campaign—that's in the hands of subordinates—

and in any event I would never let such things influence my decision. I also deeply resent the cheap shots you reporters are so fond of taking at elected officials and at hardworking businessmen, who contribute more to American life in one day than you parasites do in a year. Capital punishment is clearly intended to punish the habitual criminal, to remove permanently the unwanted elements from our society. Mr. Sockefellow's crime was one of passion and impulse. His actions are deplorable, but he in no way threatens either our safety or our well-being, and he deserves, in my humble estimation, the benefit of the doubt. The common criminal, on the other hand, deserves just what he gets."

With views in real life so closely paralleling those expressed in this hypothetical interview, it's no wonder capital punishment is not an effective deterrent to capital crime. If only a select class is subject to it and then only a small percentage of that select class actually receive it, why should anyone be afraid of Virginia Woolf?

It is frightening, however, that a majority of Americans within the past 25 years have changed their positions and now support capital punishment. Even more appalling is the fact that the size of the majority is increasing annually. Probably, this upward spiral of support will continue until the public is confronted with the stark reality that only public executions will deter criminals from partaking in beastly acts against fellow humans.

As long as capital punishment is an impersonal abnegation of respect for humanity, the masses are not compelled to demand the next logical step. What will happen, though, when the media stops treating executions by state authority as a passing fancy in this world of extreme contradiction? Now, nightly television devotes no more than thirty seconds to victims of governmental homicides, if that much. The press may add fifty lines of printed type in some obscure back-page section unless the execution was local. Then it devotes a full page, but still the episode is shortly forgotten by editor, writer, and community.

Isolation from the ritual of human sacrifice insulates the public from squarely facing the immorality of the events. To them, some unknown fiend committing some unforgivable crime got what was coming to him, and the world is better off as a result. The public is certain that the death was merciful, because our government would not do anything brutal or demeaning to humanity—and certainly wouldn't lie to us. Lack of me-

115

dia coverage, plus the propaganda hype by supporters of capital punishment, have caused the argument to be shifted from the morality of the act to the painlessness of it.

Regardless of the polls indicating the overwhelming support of Americans for capital punishment, some things are *prima facie* evidence of wrongdoing. State-sanctioned bloodletting is one of them. I stand with Henrik Ibsen, who said: "The minority is always right,"[15] later adding: "The strongest man in the world is he who stands alone."[16]

VI.

DISCRIMINATION AND CAPITAL PUNISHMENT

The penalty provides, and will always provide, the opportunity for masking racism and prejudice. Its history marches in step with the history of genocide; its cadence is the cadence of expediency; its failures, the failure of humankind.

—Capital Losses: The Price of the Death Penalty for New York State

If only about four percent of those who actually commit murders in the first degree [are executed], a figure based on what we conservatively estimate to be the number of capital murders committed annually in the United States and the accurate knowledge we have of the number of executions, it is obvious that, whatever the elements may be that produce the attrition, retribution is but rarely achieved in an equitable manner. Therefore, just as the death penalty has proved to fail as a special means of social protection, so it has failed as an instrument of retributive justice.

—Thorsten Sellin, "Capital Punishment," *Federal Probation*[1]

A simple true-or-false quiz about capital punishment should be sufficient to dispel many popularly-held notions that its application is fair and evenhanded:

1.   At least one rich person convicted of first degree murder in the United States has been executed.

117

2. All persons convicted of first-degree murder are sentenced to death or life imprisonment.

3. Most inmates on death row are Blacks.

4. All convicted felons in capital offense cases are entitled to state-compensated attorneys for appeals.

5. No state permits the execution of persons under the age of fifteen years.

6. Citizens who oppose the death penalty in principle have a legal right to sit as jurors in capital offense trials.

7. Juries that convict and agree that the punishment should be life in prison instead of execution cannot be overruled by judges.

8. At least five of the most vicious criminals in American history, those identified with organized crime such as the Mafia or the Cosa Nostra, have been executed.

If you answered all eight questions as true, you register on the scale as an imbecile. If you answered true to six of the eight, you could qualify for the idiot level. If you answered true to any question, you are hopelessly unaware of the situation surrounding capital punishment. The correct answer to all eight questions is absolutely, unequivocably **False**.

1. RACISM AND THE DEATH PENALTY

In the *Furman v. Georgia* decision of June 29, 1972, the Supreme Court held that capital punishment as administered under then-existing statutes was unconstitutional. It ruled that arbitrariness and capriciousness in the imposition of the penalty violated the Eighth Amendment prohibition against cruel and unusual punishments. Reacting to *Furman*, state legislatures enacted new capital punishment statutes attempting to remedy constitutional defects by placing restrictions on sentencing discretion. These post-*Furman* statutes took two basic approaches: the "mandatory" death sentence for certain offenses, which eliminated *all* sentencing discretion, or "guided discretion" statutes which provided explicit standards (usually in the form of aggravating and mitigating circumstances) to be followed in sentencing.

In 1976, in *Gregg v. Georgia*,[2] *Woodson v. North Carolina*,[3] and three companion cases,[4] the Supreme Court: (1) held that capital punishment for the crime of murder does not *per se* constitute cruel and unusual punishment; (2) rejected the mandatory death penalty statutes of North Carolina and Louisiana; and (3) upheld the guided discretion statutes of

Florida, Georgia, and Texas. In affirming the guided discretion statutes, the Court expressed its belief that they provide safeguards which should correct the arbitrary and capricious application of the death penalty to which the Court had objected in *Furman*.

Several tables included in the Appendix provide statistics on:

1. Persons on death row, year end (1973-1979), by race and state (Table IV);
2. Persons sentenced to death, (1973-1979), by race and state (Table V);
3. Executions by race, offense and state, 1930-1979 (Table VI);
4. Persons on death row by race, May 1, 1987 (Table VII).

Table IV presents a breakdown by race and state of the death-row population at year end for the years following the *Furman* decision through 1979. It should be noted that the figures for pre-1976 and those for 1976 through 1979 are not strictly comparable due to a change in the techniques employed by the Department of Justice in counting the number of individuals under sentence of death.

Beginning with 1976, inmates sentenced to death under statutory provisions later found unconstitutional are removed from the death row count as of the date of the relevant court finding, rather than as of the specific application of the finding to the individual, as had been the practice prior to 1976. In addition, this table excludes the "other" racial category which has consistently constituted only a very small percentage of those under sentence of death. The footnote at the bottom of the table provides the yearly breakdown of individuals in this category.

Between 1973 and 1979, thirty-five states at one time or another had individuals under sentence of death at year's end. In general, the trend has been since 1975 that the proportion of Blacks on death row has been decreasing—from 54 percent in 1975 to 39 percent in 1979. There are at least two reasons for this decrease: death penalty statutes in states with large proportions of Blacks on death row have been held unconstitutional, and the percentage of Blacks who are sentenced to death has been declining (see Table V). The trend by 1986 has begun to reverse itself, in favor of re-establishing the former pattern of racial imbalance between Blacks and whites. Blacks now represent forty-six percent of the total (see Table VII).

Due to the relatively small number of individuals under sentence of death in most states, comparisons of the percentage of whites and Blacks under sentence of death may be misleading. For example, knowing that fifty percent of two individuals under sentence of death in a state are Black does not provide much insight. However, tentative comparisons can be made using those states with more sizable death row populations. These states include: Ohio, North Carolina, Georgia, Florida, Texas, and California. As a group these states contributed between a low of forty-six percent in 1973 and a high of seventy-nine percent in 1977 of the total number under sentence of death in the nation.

Between 1973 and 1976 Blacks made up a majority of those under sentence of death in North Carolina. Since 1976 (when the North Carolina statute was declared unconstitutional), the number under sentence of death has not changed significantly. More than 50% are still Black. During this period, Georgia shows a trend of increasing percentages of Blacks on death row. In 1973 Blacks made up about 30% of those on death row in Georgia. This percentage rose to 60% in 1975 and has fluctuated around 53% since 1976. Today it is 46% (see Table VII). Florida shows a decline of Blacks as a percentage of the death row population over this time period. Today the Black death row population is 39% (see Table VII). Finally, in California between 1973 and 1975 Blacks made up about 37% of those under sentence of death. In 1976 and 1977 the percentage of inmates under sentence of death in California who were Black was 37% and 41%, respectively. This number dropped to 22% in 1979, but rose to 48% in 1986.

Table V presents a breakdown by race and state of persons who received the death penalty during the years 1973-1979. This information differs from that provided in Table IV because it includes all individuals who received the death penalty without regard to later judicial or executive action (*i.e.*, overturning of convictions, invalidating of statutes, granting of clemency, etc.). As with the figures for the year-end death row populations, the general trend has been a decline in the proportion of Blacks sentenced to death—from 66% in 1973 to 37% in 1979.

Five states account for more than half (597) of the 1,133 persons sentenced to death during these years: California, Florida, North Carolina, Ohio, and Texas. Between 1973-79, about 45% of these sentenced to death nationwide were Black. For California the proportion was about 31% black; 45% in Florida; 61% in North Carolina; 63% in Ohio; and 32% in Texas. Today those same five states have 838 death row inmates accounting for 47% of the total. When adding four other states—Alabama (83); Georgia (107); Pennsylvania (82); and Arizona (54)—the total for these nine states comes to 1,164—or 66% of the total death row inmate population (see Table VII).

One way to interpret this data is to compare the racial composition of inmates under sentence of death with the racial composition of the state population. Tables B-C give the estimated percentages of each state's Black population in 1975, compared with Black prison population.

The fact that the proportion of Blacks sentenced to death or to prison terms is larger than their proportion in a state's general population does not necessarily indicate racial discrimination in the application of the death penalty. It is possible that Blacks commit a disproportionate number of capital offenses. In fact, since 1973 the FBI has reported that approximately 50% of all those arrested for criminal homicide have been Black. Therefore, it would be reasonable to expect that half of those sentenced to death would be Black. The six states listed in Tables B-C demonstrate much larger Black prison populations than their representation in those states' populations as a whole.

These percentages are close to the percent of Blacks sentenced to death in these states. Of course it is also possible to argue that racial discrimination throughout the criminal justice process results in the disproportionate arrest, conviction, and imprisonment of Blacks, as well as disproportionate numbers sentenced to death.

There are, of course, factors which the attached tables do not take into consideration, as, for example, the circumstances surrounding a crime, or the prior records of the defendants. More importantly, the tables only compare the race of individuals who actually receive the death penalty. A more complete picture would also include information on persons charged with and convicted of capital crimes who do not receive the death penalty. Such information is not readily available.

Table VI presents the number of executions nationwide by race and offense, from 1930—the beginning date for officially-recorded statistics on executions—to 1979. During that period some 3,862 persons were executed under civil authority in the United States. Not included are 160 executions carried out by the military authority. All except three of these executions were carried out before 1967. During this period, 54% of the individuals executed were Black, 45% were white, and 1% were members of other ethnic groups. The vast majority of executions were for murder, with Blacks accounting for 49% of the total put to death for that crime. Only 12% of all executions were for rape, but nearly 90% of all persons put to death for that crime were Black.

During the time period 1930-1967, Blacks consistently represented approximately 10% of the U.S. population. Though on the face of it Blacks have been overrepresented among those executed, this fact alone does not constitute evidence of racial discrimination, as discussed above. Nearly half the executions for murder were executions of Blacks, five times the percentage of Blacks in the population—but it is generally recognized that throughout this time period Blacks had much higher homicide rates than whites—from four to ten times as high.[5]

For the crime of rape, on the other hand, the case for possible racial discrimination is stronger. As stated above, nearly 90% of all executions for rape were executions of Black males. Except for ten executions in Missouri and two under federal jurisdiction, all executions for rape took place under the jurisdiction of states in the Southern region. In five southern states and the District of Columbia, no whites were executed for rape during this period, but sixty-seven Blacks were. These statistics, along with findings of racial bias in executions for rape in several studies discussed below, indicate that with regard to the crime of rape there is a strong *prima facie* case for racial discrimination in imposition of the death penalty. However, there have been *no* executions in this country for the crime of rape since 1964. The 1977 Supreme Court case of *Coker v. Georgia*[6] held capital punishment unconsitutional for the crime of rape of an adult woman where no death results. At year's end 1979, all persons on death row had been convicted of murder, except for one defendant in Florida who was sentenced for "sexual battery of a female child age 11 or under by a male age 18 or older."

Table VIII, which was compiled by the U.S. Department of Justice, Bureau of Justice Statistics: *Bulletin on Capital Punishment*, 1985, provides seven different tables, labelled VIII-A through VIII-G: A. Profile of Capital Punishment Statutes During 1985; B. Method of Executions by State in 1985; C. Minimum Age Authorized for Capital Punishment 1985; D. Demographic Profile of Prisoners Under Sentence of Death 1985; E. Criminal History Profile of Prisoners Under Sentence of Death, by Race, in 1985; F. Percentage of Those Under Sentence of Death Executed or Received Other Dispositions, by Race, 1977-1985; and G. Elapsed Time Between Imposition of Death Sentence and Execution, by Race, 1977-1985.

The following is an examination of some of the major studies of discrimination in the imposition of the death penalty. They are divided into two groups: studies of sentencing prior to the *Furman* decision, and studies of sentencing after that decision.

2. PRE-FURMAN RESEARCH

Among the earliest studies of race and the death penalty were three conducted in the 1940s. In 1941, Guy Johnson studied homicide indictments, convictions, and sentences in selected counties in Georgia, North Carolina, and Virginia for the period 1930-1940. Johnson collected information on the race of victims as well as offenders. Johnson's data was not complete,[7] but with respect to five counties in North Carolina he found that the likelihood of a death sentence following an indictment for criminal homicide varied substantially by offender/victim racial combinations. Of 141 Black offender/Black victim cases, there were eight sentences of life imprisonment and no death sentences. Of twenty-two Black offender/white victim cases, seven defendants received life imprisonment and six received the death penalty. The quality and quantity of the data precluded further analysis, but Johnson concluded that:

> Negro versus Negro offenses are treated with undue leniency, while the Negro versus white offenses are treated with undue severity.[8]

Although this conclusion accurately reflects Johnson's findings, the small size of his sample and his lack of consideration of other variables preclude making any strong inferences from his results.

Similar results were reached by Harold Garfinkel in a study published in 1949, in which he examined the progress of criminal homicide cases through successive stages of the criminal justice process in North Carolina for the years 1930-1940. He found differential treatment according to race of offender and victim at the indictment, charging, and conviction stages of the criminal justice process.[9] The third study in this period was by Charles Mangum, who in 1940 reported that for each of nine Southern and border states during the 1920s and 1930s, commutations of death sentences were more likely for whites than for Blacks.[10]

While these early studies suggested that there were significant differences according to race of offenders and victims in the administration of capital punishment in several Southern and border states, they did not take into account the possibility that the crimes of Blacks or the crimes against whites were more serious or aggravated in nature, and therefore, were more likely to result in a death penalty. The first study that attempted to consider variables related to the circumstance of the crime was conducted with data on death row inmates in Pennsylvania for the period 1914-1958. Wolfgang, Kelly, and Nolde examined the possibility that higher execution rates for Blacks occurred because Black condemned murderers were more likely than whites to have committed felony murders (*i.e.*, murders committed during the course of another crime) for which commutations were less apt to be granted. They found it to be true that Blacks were more likely than whites to have committed felony murders, but they also found that Blacks were less likely than whites to receive commutations for *non*-felony murders as well.[11] No circumstances of the crime other than the commission of contemporaneous felonies were taken into account by this study, nor was the race of the victims.

A more extensive effort to examine the racial factor in capital sentencing was undertaken by Wolfgang and his associates in 1965. They gathered data on some 3,000 convicted rapists in selected counties of eleven Southern and border states in which rape was a capital offense for the period 1945-65. The study was sponsored by the NAACP Legal Defense Fund and was conducted by the Center for Studies in Criminology and Criminal Law at the University of Pennsylvania.

The study examined only those defendants who actually were convicted of rape. It did not consider whether Blacks more frequently than whites commit rape, or whether they are more frequently arrested and charged. The study addressed only the following question: Among convicted defendants is it possible to determine whether Black defendants are disproportionately sentenced to death, and, if so, can the disproportion be explained by nonracial variables?

The researchers collected data on the race of defendants and victims, and also other information about many nonracial variables that could be construed as mitigating or aggravating circumstances. Their findings showed, firstly, that the death sentence was more likely for Blacks than for whites, and especially so for Blacks whose victims were white. The researchers estimated that Black defendants whose victims were white were sentenced to death approximately eighteen times more frequently than defendants in any other racial combination of defendant and victim.[12] Secondly, of over two dozen possibly aggravating nonracial variables tested (*e.g.*, prior convictions, use of force, commission of contemporaneous felonies, etc.), none could be found to be accountable for the disproportionate number of Blacks sentenced to death for rape.[13]

In a later study which re-analyzed the data for Georgia only, Wolfgang and Riedel employed a statistical method (discriminant analysis) which allowed them to examine the effects of fourteen different variables simultaneously, rather than one at a time. Discriminant analysis attempts to distinguish between groups based on the characteristics of individuals within the groups. In this study, the researchers' concern was with identifying characteristics which would place an individual into the death sentence group or the non-death sentence group. Wolfgang and Riedel found that the racial combination of defendant and victim, as well as the commission of contemporaneous felonies and the year of sentence, were important factors in distinguishing the individuals in the two groups. Their analysis indicated that it was the relationship of the race of the offender and the victim in combination which was significant rather than the race of either singly in determining which individuals received the death penalty for rape in Georgia. These results supported the findings of the earlier analysis.[14]

Finally, a 1969 study examined social class as well as race as a basis for differential sentencing. The study analyzed the sentences of 238 persons convicted in California of first-degree murder between 1958 and 1966. Race of victim and offender were not found to be significantly related to the likelihood of death sentence, but the investigation found that by occupation, "blue collar" defendants were more likely and "white collar" defendants less likely, to be sentenced to death.[15] Over the eight-year period, 42% of blue collar workers convicted of murder received death sentences, while the comparable figure for white collar workers was 5%. The study concluded, after taking account of other factors such as previous criminal record, that low socio-economic status made it more likely that a defendant would be sentenced to death.[16] Once again, because of the small size of the sample used in this study, no significant inferences can be supported statistically by these results.

3. POST-FURMAN RESEARCH

One of the earliest studies of the racial factor in sentencing under post-*Furman* statutes was conducted by Marc Riedel. He compared the racial composition of offenders sentenced to death in the pre-*Furman* era with those sentenced under the new statutes enacted following that decision. The pre-*Furman* population used by Riedel consisted of 493 offenders under sentence of death in twenty-eight states as of December 31, 1971. The post-*Furman* population consisted of 145 offenders under sentence of death on January 2, 1976.

Riedel determined that a larger proportion of non-whites had been sentenced to death under post-*Furman* than under pre-*Furman* statutes. To determine which states accounted for the increase he grouped the states into four regions, and determined that with the exception of the Southern region, where the proportion of non-whites had shown a small insignificant decrease, the other regions of the country all had larger proportions of non-whites under sentence of death. He found that the Western region contributed most to the increase.[17]

Riedel then attempted to determine whether there were any differences between post-*Furman* mandatory and guided discretion states (Florida, Georgia, and Texas) and three mandatory states (Louisiana, North Carolina, and Oklahoma). He found no significant differences in either the mandatory or guided discretion states.[18] From his analysis Riedel concluded:

> There is no evidence to suggest that post-Furman statutes have been successful in reducing the discretion which leads to a disproportionate number of nonwhite offenders being sentenced to death.[19]

The limitations of Riedel's findings should be noted. Like earlier studies which relied on simple tabular comparisons, Riedel only examined the influence of two factors in his analysis—race of offender and geographic location. In addition, the number of individuals within each geographic region, or within the "guided discretion" or "mandatory sentence" states, was quite small. As a result, in some instances Riedel was unable to apply statistical tests to his findings. Therefore, any inferences deriving from his findings should be viewed as tentative. However, Riedel's findings do gain support from later work by William J. Bowers and Glenn F. Pierce.

Bowers and Pierce undertook an extensive examination of capital sentencing in selected states for the first five years following *Furman*. Their analysis examined five potential sources of arbitrariness in application of the death penalty: (1) arbitrariness by race; (2) arbitrariness by place; (3) arbitrariness by stages of the criminal justice process; (4) arbitrariness and the judicial review process; and (5) arbitrariness and form of the law. The results of their analysis are discussed below.

4. ARBITRARINESS BY RACE

Bowers and Pierce first examined the likelihood of a death sentence for homicide by offender/victim racial categories in Florida, Georgia, Texas, and Ohio.[20] Table D (see the Appendix) presents their estimate of the total number of criminal offenders, the number of persons sentenced to death, and the probability or likelihood of a death sentence for each offender/victim racial combination in each of the four states from the effective date of their post-*Furman* statutes through 1977.

Bowers and Pierce based their analysis on the estimated number of criminal homicides, rather than a sample of indictments as other researchers had done, in an attempt to span the entire criminal justice process and incorporate the effects of discretion at every stage in the handling of potentially capital cases—from the initial investigation of the crime through arrest, charging, indictment, conviction, and sentencing. Their data (see Table D) shows a consistent pattern across all four states: Black killers, and the killers of whites, are more likely than white killers and the killers of Blacks to receive the death penalty. These results are similar to those obtained in the earlier studies discussed above regarding sentencing under pre-*Furman* statutes.

Bowers and Pierce then attempted to determine whether the racial differences were a result of the direct influence of race, or whether there were other legally relevant differences in the kinds of crimes committed by and against Blacks and whites. For the states of Florida, Georgia, and Texas, they examined the chance of a death sentence by race of offender and victim separately for two categories of murder: felony murder (which by definition qualifies for the death penalty in all three states) and non-felony murder (which may or may not qualify). Their data showed that type of murder did not account for racial differences in the probability of receiving the death penalty. For both felony and non-felony homicides, the same differences by race of both offender and victim appeared.[21]

5. ARBITRARINESS BY PLACE

For this part of their analysis, Bowers and Pierce examined the likelihood of a death sentence according to judicial circuits grouped regionally within Florida and Georgia, from the effective dates of their respective post-*Furman* capital statutes through 1977. Their results are presented in Table E (see the Appendix).

In Florida, the table indicates that a death sentence is nearly two and one-half times more likely in the panhandle area than in the southern portion of the state, with the northern and central regions falling in between. In Georgia, a death sentence in the central region is over six times more likely than in the northern region, and between seven and eight times as likely in the central region as in Fulton County (which includes Atlanta). However, although there is a substantial difference in the *relative* probability of receiving a death sentence in different areas within each state, the actual difference in the percentages is quite small. The probability of death among the different areas ranges from 2.0% to 4.8% in Florida, and in Georgia from .7% to 4.5%. If one considers the differences between the percentages involved rather than the ratio of one probability to another, the differences between the geographical regions could be considered quite small.

Because differences among the regions could be reflective of regional variations in the kind of homicides committed, Bowers and Pierce attempted to take this factor into consideration by breaking the homicides down according to felony and non-felony circumstances. Their findings showed that the regional differences were independent of the felony/non-felony classification.

6. ARBITRARINESS BY STAGES OF THE PROCESS

Next Bowers and Pierce examined several stages in the criminal justice process, in an attempt to determine whether the effects of race and location are concentrated at a particular point, or whether they are pervasive throughout the process. The data studied related to the processing of potentially capital cases in selected counties of Florida. Several decision points were examined: the decision to bring first degree versus lesser homicide charges; the decision to convict for first degree murder versus acquit or convict on a lesser charge; and the decision to impose the death penalty versus a lesser penalty for persons convicted of first degree murder. The research revealed that at each stage of the process, the race of both the offender and the victim affected the defendant's chances of moving to the next stage. They also found that race not only influenced movement from one stage to the next, but also affected decisions within certain stages of the criminal justice process— *i.e.*, decisions about whether to introduce felony-related cirumstances in case records, whether to charge an accompanying felony at trial, and whether to find an aggravating felony circumstance at sentencing.[22]

Bowers and Pierce recognized that their data could be subject to challenge,[23] because it comes from a selected sample of cases not chosen to be representative of the whole state of Florida, and because it was collected by persons associated with a group opposing capital punishment. However, they justified their analysis as useful, because the data was the only post-*Furman* information available relating to the processing of capital cases. They also expressed their belief that the data was not prejudiced by the point of view of those who collected it, because the information was gathered under the supervision of professional social scientists. And they pointed out that the findings from this data were consistent with data from earlier studies, such as that of Garfinkel in the 1940s.

7. ARBITRARINESS AND APPELLATE REVIEW

In this portion of their analysis, Bowers and Pierce tabulated the outcomes of appellate review of death sentences imposed in Florida and Georgia from the effective date of their statutes through 1977. They examined the probability of affirmation given information on the race of offenders and victims and the location within the state. Ninety-one appellate review cases were identified for Florida and ninety for Georgia. Their findings showed that after appellate review in both states, the offender/victim racial categories stood in virtually the same relationship to one another as they did before appellate review, leading them to conclude that "There is no tendency for the appellate review process to correct the racial differences in treatment."[24] They also did not find any indication that the appellate review process adjusted regional difference.[25]

8. ARBITRARINESS AND FORM OF THE LAW

In this section of the study, Bowers and Pierce tabulated the aggravating circumstances found for all cases in Georgia and Florida on which reliable information was available. Florida and Georgia have capital statutes with similar lists of aggravating circumstances. However, in Georgia the jury needs to find only one such circumstance to recommend death, while in Florida aggravated circumtances must "outweigh" mitigating circumstances. Therefore, Bowers and Pierce hypothesized that if imposition of the death penalty is based on extralegal factors, then Florida courts should find more aggravating circumstances than Georgia courts. In fact, they found that on the average there were twice as many aggravating circumstances reported for Florida as compared with Georgia cases receiving the death penalty. From a further analysis of the specific aggravating factors found in each state, they concluded that "sentencing guidelines become the instrument of arbitrariness and discrimination, not their cure."[26]

Based on the results of their five separate analyses, Bowers and Pierce concluded:

In the first five years after the Furman decision, racial differences in the administration of capital statutes have been extreme in magnitude, similar across states and under different statutory forms, pervasive over successive stages of the judicial process, and uncorrected by appellate review. Moreover, these differentials have been fully consistent with the pattern of racial disparity occurring under capital statutes invalidated by the Furman decision....

We have also seen substantial differentials in treatment by judicial circuits within states under different kinds of capital statutes, evident at discrete stages of the criminal justice process and unaltered by appellate review. And, we have established that the observed differences by judicial circuits within a state are quite independent of race of offender and victim, and hence an entirely separate source of differential treatment under post-*Furman* capital statutes.[27]

While the Bowers and Pierce analysis is extensive in its scope, its findings must be viewed in context. Firstly, the analysis relies on data from organizations that may not be experienced in the collection of data of this type. Secondly, important portions of the analysis rest upon estimates of the number of offenders within a particular offender/victim category. If these estimates are significantly different than the actual number of offenders within each category, the results would be altered. Thirdly, Bowers and Pierce group together all the data from the years studied, so that there is no indication whether discrimination that might have occurred in one year has changed over time. Finally, the examination of data from more states, as well as the use of more sophisticated statistical techniques, would be needed in order to make strong inferences from their findings.

Unlike the deterrence issue over which there is great debate, the literature on discrimination and the death penalty is in nearly total agreement that there has been racial discrimination in the imposition of the death penalty.

The studies from the post-*Furman* era are perhaps the most relevant to the capital punishment debate today, but it should be remembered that the most recent of these studies ended with data for the year 1977. Since that year the Supreme Court has continued to scrutinize the way in which the states apply the death penalty, and has issued several rulings refining and narrowing the scope of its use. Also, since 1977 the proportion of Blacks on death row has been steadily decreasing. A more complete picture of capital sentencing in the post-*Furman* era would include an analysis of the data for the years following 1977.

Such an analysis was conducted by Professor David Baldus of the University of Iowa's Law School, and presented to the courts in the *Warren McCleskey v. Ralph M. Kemp* case. His study revealed that in the state of Georgia between 1973 and 1979, 973 persons arrested for killing whites received 108 death sentences. During the same period of time, in the same state, only twenty of 1,502 persons arrested for killing Blacks were sentenced to death. He also documented that fifty of 228 Blacks arrested for killing whites received death, while fifty-eight of 745 whites arrested for killing whites were similarly sentenced. In simple terms, Georgians accused of killing a white man are eleven times more likely to receive the death penalty than those accused of killing Blacks. It also attests to the fact that Blacks are three times more likely to receive the death sentence for killing whites than whites who kill whites.

The McCleskey case involved the murder of a white Atlanta police officer during a burglary at a furniture store. He answered an alarm at the store and was shot by one of four men who were fleeing the scene. McCleskey admitted a role in the burglary, but denied shooting the policeman. One of his cohorts in the crime testified that McCleskey was the gunman, and a prison cellmate attempting to make a deal with the prosecution for early release testified that McCleskey told him that he pulled the trigger. He was convicted and sentenced to death. The Appeals Court upheld the conviction and his case was taken to the Supreme Court.

The Congressional Black Caucus, at the request of Rep. John Conyers, filed an *amicus curiae* brief before the Supreme Court in the case of Warren McCleskey. Also joining in the brief were the Lawyers' Committee for Civil Rights Under Law, and the National Association for the Advancement of Colored People.

The brief held that:

> The unequal application of criminal statutes on the basis of race is a violation of the Constitution, and yet the Court of Appeals ruled that a proven racial disparity in death sentencing did not in and of itself violate the Eighth and Fourteenth Amendments.

The scientific evidence in this case tests every possible explanation for these apparent disparities, and showed nothing to explain them but the conscious or unconscious influence of race.

There was no justification for imposing proof of an intentional act of discrimination since the strong statistical proof presented, coupled with a history of discrimination, sufficiency showed "purposeful discrimination."

Since *Gregg v. Georgia*, the state of Georgia had carried out seven executions, six of them were Blacks convicted of killing whites. Of the fifteen men under death sentences presently, thirteen were Black; nine of them convicted of killing whites.

The Court of Appeals gave two basic reasons for rejecting McCleskey's argument: the supposedly insignificant magnitude of the racial disparities; and the lack of direct proof of a discriminatory motive.

In a sense, the Court agreed that racial bias played a part in the conviction, but just not enough bias to warrant a reversal. It ruled that statistical proof of racial bias "is insufficient to invalidate a capital sentencing system, unless that disparate impact is so great that it compels a conclusion that the system is unprincipled, irrational, arbitrary, and capricious such that purposeful discrimination—*i.e.*, race, is intentionally being used as a factor...."[28]

But the question Professor Baldus does not and cannot answer is whether the impact of race on Georgia's death sentencing system is the result of deliberate discrimination or unconscious racial influence on the actors who are part of it.

The study certainly demonstrates that race is a significant influence in sentencing. The Court of Appeals and, subsequently, the U.S. Supreme Court ruled that this pattern affronts no constitutional principles, although Baldus's findings were both comprehensive and exhaustive, as described in the *New Republic*:

With the scientific precision of an epidermiologist seeking to pinpoint the cause of a new disease, Baldus analyzed and reanalyzed his mountain of data on Georgia homicides, controlling for the hundreds of variables in each case, in search of any explanation other than race which might account for the stark inequalities in Georgia's capital sentencing system. He could find none.[29]

Requiring proof of subjective intent in the sentencing context raises an impossible burden, the *New Republic* editorial concluded.

Justice Brennan, writing for the Supreme Court minority in the McCleskey case, said:

> It is tempting to pretend that minorities on death row share a fate in no way connected to our own, that our treatment of them sounds no echoes beyond the chambers in which they die. Such an illusion is ultimately corrosive, for the reverberations of injustice are not so easily confined....The way in which we choose those who will die reveals the depth of moral commitment among the living.[30]

Proof of pervasive economic and racial discrimination in dispensing capital punishment sentences is apparent to all knowledgeable persons except a majority on the Supreme Court. All honest people willingly admit that the death penalty is primarily applied in the South, to Blacks and poor whites, by an aristocracy which is obsessed with a fervent desire to keep Blacks and poor whites in their places.

Proponents of capital punishment tout the "need" to preserve life and maintain social order. Neither goal is necessarily enhanced by officially-sanctioned state executions, nor does pursuit of either objective explain why only the poor are victimized by it. Our national myths do not allow us to admit the disgraceful truth about capital punishment. Primitive visions of medieval torture chambers are deliberately screened from our view by slick public relations ploys. Such propaganda convinces the average American that executions are somehow humane, civilized, and painless ways of ridding our society of its unpleasant mistakes and misfits.

Our national failure to understand these inherent class and racial biases is intertwined with two hundred years of official hypocrisy, which has intentionally and systematically denigrated, demeaned and devalued the worth of poor people and minorities. The Declaration of Independence and the Constitution obviously do not realistically address the problems of race, sex, or poverty. In fact, the drafters of these eloquent statements, inscribed for posterity on unbleached parchments, prohibited white women the use of the ballot, denied poor white men who owned no property the right to vote, and sanctioned slavery of Black people. These attitudes reflected the ideas of the time.

Our present national mind-set has its genesis in the ideas contained in the Declaration of Independence and the Constitution. Both documents favored property rights over human rights. Both regarded some in our society not truly human in the fullest sense of the word. The counting of slaves as three-fifths of a person for the purpose of congressional representation is only a small manifestation of this country's early duplicity in dealing fairly with racial, sexual, and economic issues. Two hundred years of such indoctrination have reduced and pulled our sensitivity toward discrimination and related topics.

Our system of criminal justice was not intentionally designed to protect the rich and punish the poor. Correction officers, police, juries, judges, and prosecutors were not originally seen as enemies of any special class. In fact, just the opposite was envisioned by our founding fathers. The establishment of these mechanisms was designed for the express purpose of guaranteeing every person a swift, fair trial, affording them the protections of due process and presumption of innocence. Unfortunately, the ideal was never realized in practice.

By a vote of 5 to 4, the Supreme Court recently held that a study detailing statistical evidence of more than 2,000 murder cases in Georgia found that Black men were 4.3 times as likely to receive capital punishment as whites who killed Blacks. But the Court also rationalized the disparity as "a discrepancy that appears to correlate with race," and further stated that such "apparent disparities in sentencing are an inevitable part of our criminal justice system."[31]

Justice Blackmun asserted in the case of Warren McCleskey of Georgia that evidence indicated "a clear pattern of differential treatment according to race."[32]

Justice Powell concurred that "apparent disparities in sentencing, whether or not racial, will happen. They always have, they always will, they can't be prevented—and no better reason exists for doing away with the one sentence that cannot be revoked or redeemed, once it has been carried out."

This callous attitude about racial and economic disparity is pervasive among judges at all levels. While the rate of executions for Blacks is disproportionate to their numbers, the number of poor whites being executed are also increasing. During the last fifty years, of all persons executed in this country, 54% have been Black and 45% poor whites. If a person is both a minority and impoverished, his chances of execution following conviction of a capital offense are more than four times as great as that of a middle-class white.

Only 30% of the American population is officially classified as poor, but 95% of those on death row are poor. Only 12% of the nation's population is Black, but 65% of all Blacks fall below the poverty line. If 95% of all the criminals on death row fall into the category of poor, and 41% of them are Black, then simple logic tells us that a felon who is both poor and Black runs a greater risk of being executed than those in the average criminal population.

9. THE VICTIMS OF CAPITAL PUNISHMENT

...Any man's death diminishes me, because I am involved in mankind; and therefore never send to know for whom the bell tolls; it tolls for thee.

—John Donne[33]

Available public studies show the capricious and arbitrary manner in which the death penalty has been imposed in the United States. Between the years 1930-1985, almost four thousand persons were officially executed by federal and state agencies (see Table VI in the Appendix). The only constant factor in each case was that every victim, virtually without exception, came from an economically disadvantaged or a minority group, or both. Poverty and race are the two controlling components of the capital punishment equation. Ethics, principles, or morality hardly ever influence the state's decision to kill people. The crime itself does not dictate when the penalty shall be applied. If it did, then the rich, the famous, the influential would have occasionally suffered this most harsh of punishments. They have not, and will not as long as its possible to buy or manipulate the legal system. Retribution for their crimes range from life in prison, in the most extreme cases, to outright exoneration—depending on the depth of their pocketbooks, the notoriety of their fame, or the pervasiveness of their influence.

Note was duly taken of this imperfection in the system during Supreme Court deliberations of the *Furman v. Georgia* (1972) case. Justice Douglas said, "One searches our chronicles in vain for the execution of any member of the affluent strata of this society. The Leopolds and Loebs are given prison terms, not sentenced to death."[34] Leopold and Loeb were rich young men who killed for the expressed purpose of experiencing the thrill of doing it. A famous criminal lawyer, Clarence Darrow, represented them in court, and was able to convince the judge to spare their lives by giving them life in prison.

To comprehend the extent and magnitude of the capital punishment problem in the U.S., one must add to the official list of 3,959 victims officially executed the thousands of Blacks illegally lynched prior to 1950. Although these hangings were not in accordance with law, they were just as lethal, and just as legal, because the law never challenged the right of whites to pursue this course of action. Seldom, if ever, was anyone prosecuted for taking the law into his hands. The prevailing attitude of official white governments was, "The nigger deserved it."

After 1934, lynchings declined drastically, and have not constituted a problem of national import for some decades. Between 1935-1962, only eighty-five persons were classified as lynching victims. But prior to that time, from 1882-1934, 4,736 people, most of them Blacks, were recorded in official documents as victims of mob hangings. Imagine the thousands of unidentified victims, many of them wholly innocent of their alleged crimes, whose bodies lie mouldering in the ground. Of the official number, 3,362 were Blacks accused of homicides, felonious assault, rape, attempted rape, robbery, theft, or "insult" to white persons.

Following the Civil War, white hate groups sprang up across the South, determined to deny Blacks their rights of citizenship. They used terrorist methods to impose their own brand of justice on Blacks. The official number of lynchings may be understated by as much as 75%, since most never came to public attention, and those which did were quickly noted as necessary actions to preserve law and order—*i.e.*, "to keep the niggers down."

James Weldon Johnson, field secretary of the National Association for the Advancement of Colored People, assigned to investigate the lynching of Eli Persons, a Black man burned to death in Memphis, wrote the following:

> On the day I arrived in Memphis, Robert R. Church drove me out to the place where the burning had taken place. A pile of ashes and pieces of charred wood still marked the spot. While the ashes were yet hot, the bones had been scrambled for as souvenirs by the mob. I reassembled the picture in my mind; he is chained to a stake, wood is piled under and around him, and five thousand men and women with babies in their arms, and women with babies in their wombs, look on with pitiless anticipation, with sadistic satisfaction while he is baptized with gasoline and set afire. The mob disperses, many of them complaining, "They burned him

too fast." I tried to balance the sufferings of the miserable victim against the moral degradation of Memphis, and the truth flashed over me that in large measure the race question involves the saving of Black America's body and white America's soul.[35]

One case, typical of many others, did somehow make its way to the Supreme Court of the United States, in the matter of *Moore v. Dempsey*, 261 U.S. 86 (February 19, 1923). Justice Holmes delivered the opinion. It was highly unusual that the case ever got this far, since most similar actions were disposed of by local grand juries or state authorities. But in this instance, according to the *Negro Almanac*, the case

> ...was an outgrowth of an Arkansas race riot, during which one white man was killed, and several people of both races were injured. Twelve Blacks were sentenced to death, and 67 to lengthy prison terms.
> Black witnesses appearing at the trial were whipped until they consented to testify against the accused. The all-white jury heard the case in the presence of a mob threatening violence if there were no convictions. The court-appointed counsel did not ask for a change of venue, and called no witnesses—not even the defendants themselves. The trial lasted 45 minutes, and the jury brought in a verdict of guilty after five minutes.
> NAACP attorneys later applied for a writ of *habeas corpus* in the federal courts, a petition which was at first dismissed on demurrer. The U.S. Supreme Court ultimately ruled that the petition should be heard, and reversed the decision of the Arkansas District Court, with Justice Holmes stating in his opinion that "...counsel, jury and judge were swept to the fatal end by an irresistible wave of public passion...."[36]

Conditions and circumstances really have not changed all that much since the days of legally sanctioned lynchings. Today we mouth brave words about equality, but underneath the facade the same discriminatory mentality exists toward minorities. Because Blacks and poor whites have traditonally voted in numbers disproportionately less than their real population, they remain largely without political clout. Now, of course, every step of the legal process is meticulously observed: rules, regulations, or legal safeguards may be bent, but never broken, since to do so would discredit the legal process entirely. But if we have become more careful as a society, we have yet to achieve equality, particularly where capital punishment is concerned.

Common sense tells us that there is something seriously awry with a legal system which penalizes economic and racial minorities while treating the "better" segments of society with kid gloves. If one accepts the arguments of the supporters of capital punishment (and I do not), then one must also accept the principle that this most final of judgments should be equally applied to *all* elements of American society. Until and unless this problem is rectified, the claims of proponents are and must be wholly spurious, and all executions should be suspended immediately. The Constitution expressly forbids cruel and unusual punishment; is it "usual" to apply a harsh sentence solely to one economic and/or social group? I hardly think so.

By the end of 1987, almost 2,000 convicts awaited execution in thirty-two states. Fifty percent of them (944) were white; 41% (777) Black; 5.8% (110) Hispanic; and 2.26% (34) members of other races. Only nineteen of the total were female.

It's not so strange, however, that more than 55% of the total on death row are located in a group of Southern states which account for only a small percentage of the total population. Neither is it a concidence that more than 55% of the total number of Blacks on death row are in these same eleven Southern states. Of twenty-five persons executed in 1987, all but one (in Utah) were in the South (eight in Louisiana; six in Texas; five in Georgia; two in Mississippi; and one each in Alabama, Florida, and Virginia).

Testifying before a congressional committee, Assistant Attorney General Stephen Trott attempted to make a case that race was not a factor in imposing the death sentence. He said:

> Seven of the first eight executions after the 1976 decisions beginning to rewrite the death penalty, were in fact of white murderers. Of the 47 persons executed since 1976, 28 have been white, 17 black, and 2 Hispanics. Although whites account for less than 40% of the murderers, they account for more than 60% of those executed for murder. According to the Justice Department's Bureau of Justice Statistics, for every

1,000 whites arrested on a charge of murder, almost 16 went to prison under the sentence of death. Fewer than 12 Blacks for every thousand arrested were sent to death row.[37]

What Mr. Trott failed to mention was that four of the seven whites executed after the 1976 decision voluntarily accepted the penalty: Gary Gilmore in Utah, January 17, 1977; Jesse Bishop in Nevada, October 22, 1979; Steven Judy in Indiana, March 9, 1981; and Frank Coppols in Virginia, August 10, 1982. All refused to appeal their cases and asked that their sentences be carried out.

If the figures enunciated by Mr. Trott do anything, they buttress the argument that American society places very little (if any) value on the lives of Blacks. All twenty-eight whites who were executed killed other whites. All seventeen Blacks executed were guilty of killing whites. The two Hispanics were also executed for killing whites. If more Blacks are murdered each year than whites, where is the new "get tough" policy for those who kill Blacks? The fact that so few Blacks arrested for killing other Blacks are sentenced to death is in itself an absurdity.

This attitude is exemplified in a published work by Raymond Fosdick, studying Southern police departments. He observed that there were three kinds of murder, and that they were vividly expressed by a white police officer who said,

> "If a nigger kills a white man, that's murder. If a white man kills a nigger, that's justifiable homicide. If a nigger kills another nigger, that's one less nigger."[38]

Similar conclusions have been reached by others regarding the criminal justice system's relative leniency in dealing with Black-on-Black crimes. Primarily, many of these commentators say, this kind of attitude results from society's utter contempt for the sanctity of Black lives. Edward D. Sargent, a columnist for the *Washington Post*, has stated:

> I do not write about black-on-black homicide from the vantage point of a detached observer. My black skin, my 1958 birth certificate and my male gender make me part of an endangered group. Personally, I'd rather have cancer. Currently, about 95% of murdered black males between 15 and 34 are killed by other young black

139

males, which is as disheartening as it is hard to believe. These men who call each other "brother" are killing each other faster than any disease, including AIDS, cancer, sickle cell anemia and high blood pressure....A terrible thing has happened to me and my black brothers. But nobody cares.[39]

Hortense Powdermaker, a white anthropologist, explains it differently. In her book, *After Freedom*, she says:

When a white man kills a Negro, it is hardly considered murder. When a Negro kills a white man, conviction is assured, provided the case is not settled immediately by lynch law.

The mildness of the courts where offenses of Negroes against Negroes are concerned is only part of the whole situation which places the Negro outside the law. It may be viewed as one result of the system which treats the Negro as sub-human and therefore places less value on his life than on that of a white person, and exacts less punishment for destroying it. The reinforcement of an economic motive toward leniency is suggested in the case where a good plantation hand was not prosecuted for killing another Negro. In part also, reluctance to exact a penalty for intra-Negro crime belongs to the policy which by way of "sop" or compensation indulges the Negro whenever license on his part does not infringe on white privileges. Such a policy finds support in the paternalistic white attitude which views Negros as children—irresponsible, volatile, unaccountable.[40]

In the state of South Carolina, 75% of those sentenced to die between 1977-1981 were Black—but not a single Black served on any of the juries that convicted them. That fact alone graphically highlights the problem of fairness in applying the death sentence in the United States today. As David Bruck reported in the *New Republic*:

In South Carolina, where I practice law, murders committed during robberies may be punished by death. According to police reports, there were 286 defendants arrested for such murders from the time the South Carolina death penalty law went into effect in 1977 until the end of 1981. (About a third of those arrests were of Blacks charged with killing whites.) Out of all of those 286 defendants, the prosecution had sought the death penalty and obtained final convictions by the end of 1981 against 37. And of those 37 defendants, death sentences were imposed and affirmed on only 4; the rest received prison sentences. What distinguished those 4 defendants' cases was this: 3 were Black, had killed white storeowners, and were tried by all-white juries; the fourth, a white, was represented at his trial by a lawyer who had never read the state's murder statute, had no case file and no office, and had refused to talk to his client for the last two months prior to the trial because he'd been insulted by the client's unsuccessful attempt to fire him.[41]

Day after day this same masquerade continues to be played out in the thirty-eight states that have legalized capital punishment. Incompetent, unconcerned attorneys parade into courtrooms across this nation ill-prepared to defend clients accused of capital offenses.

The excessive penalties meted out to Black criminals often result in the development of a fatalistic mind-set among this group. Many believe that killing eye witnesses is necessary to avoid being caught and executed; others would rather die in violent shoot-outs with the police, thereby permanently resting their cases in the hands of six Black pall-bearers, rather than leave their fates up to twelve white jurors.

This cynical attitude can also determine whom and under what circumstances they kill. Knowing full well that the life of a Black person has little value to many whites, particularly those with conservative views (and those advocating capital punishment), they instinctively choose as their victims other Blacks. Very few murderers of Black people have ever actually been executed. As Julian Bond, former state senator from Georgia, said, "If you are contemplating murder, better kill a Black person. You'll have a better chance of escaping the death penalty."[42]

A study conducted in the states of Georgia, Florida, and Texas for the years 1973-1977 found that of 200 death row cases, 40% were Blacks who had killed whites; 10% were Blacks who had killed other

Blacks; and 50% were whites who had killed other whites. No whites who had killed Blacks during this period ended up on death row.

The social status of the accused has, does, and will contine to play a major role in determining who is actually executed by the government. No person of means has ever gone to the electric chair or the gas chamber, although many have committed heinous (and well-publicized) crimes. The victims of capital punishment are the uneducated, the under-privileged, the financially unsuccessful. The affluent, the professional criminal, the politically well-placed, come into the court room (if at all; many avoid such appearances altogether) with a distinct advantage.

Playwright Paul Green has stated that the death penalty is "wraught against the poor, the murky-minded, the unfortunate."[43] Mr. Green is seconded by Lewis E. Lawes, former warden of Sing Sing Prison in New York State:

> In the twelve years of my wardenship, I have escorted one hundred fifty men and one woman to the death chamber and the electric chair. In ages, they ranged from seventeen to sixty-three. In only one respect were they all alike. All of them were poor and most of them were friendless.[44]

The disadvantaged, victims of the remnants of a Calvinistic mind-set, are patsies of a system primed to make examples of them to the rest of society. Because they are poor, no one feels particularly sorry for them. Where is thy pity? Where is the "Christian" love so touted by the television preachers? Where is America's heart and soul?

The poor and friendless are at the mercy of unsympathetic judges, insensitive prosecutors, hostile juries, uncaring media personalities, and ill-prepared court-appointed public defenders. "Ill-prepared," in this instance, does not always mean lack of ability or experience or desire, but often a general lack of funds and resources to hire investigative staff and to conduct research. A lawyer, no matter how competent, must be able to investigate the backgrounds of potential jurors and potential witnesses, to examine alibis, to secure experts to interpret evidence and provide testimony in court. No court-appointed attorney in the United States is provided with such resources, which are routine adjuncts to the big law offices. Therefore, the impoverished accused, who must make do with appointed legal representation, is doomed from the very beginning. He has no reasonable chance whatever of a fair trial.

Coverage by the media (radio, television, newspapers) often determines the fate of the accused long before he or she enters the court room. The fairness of such coverage depends on the responsiblity of individual reporters and publications/stations. Sadly, some are more than willing to emphasize the sensational elements of such stories, a factor which can definitely play a major role in the ultimate outcome of verdicts. As Justice Felix Frankfurter observed in *Irvin v. Dowd*:

> How can fallible men and women reach a disinterested verdict based exclusively on what they heard in court when, before they entered the jury box, their minds were saturated by press and radio for months preceding by matter designed to establish the guilt of the accused. A conviction so secured obviously constitutes a denial of due process of law in its most rudimentary conception.[45]

Reporting by newspapers, magazines, and television/radio sometimes creates a climate for dealing with the powerful in a manner differently than with the dispossessed. Human interest stories about the rich and famous can taint the process of justice. The public has been conditioned by the media to see such individuals as incapable of outrageous criminal behavior, thus rendering the selection of an impartial jury difficult, if not impossible. The notion that "refined" people are somehow better than the rest, that they do not, for example, kill for revenge or profit or power, also plays a role in explaining why they are never sent to the gallows. Courts tend to rule in their favor. They wear the "right" clothes and say the "right" things before juries. They make a "good impression." The disadvantaged, on the other hand, appear less respectable than the average juror, more "capable" of committing the crimes of which they are accused. No matter how gifted or skilled a defense attorney may be, he or she is at an immediate disadvantage when representing the poor. Is it any wonder that jurists often have problems reaching a verdict that establishes a rich defendant's guilt beyond a reasonable doubt?

The argument that the affluent and politically powerful escape the death penalty simply because they can afford to hire competent, experienced, well-compensated legal counsel is a truism, but still remains only a partial explanation. Personal familiarity with judges and prosecutors oftentimes results in sympathetic consideration at the initial stages of investigations, at coroners' inquests, in the filing of charges, or in the issuance of indictments for lesser charges, including justifiable homicide, self-defense, or no true bills. Without such influence (which poorer people generally do not have), the reality might well have been first-degree murder and/or the possibility of a death sentence.

From the initial arrest to the jury's final verdict, the legal process is so slanted against minorities and the poor that any fair consideration is extraordinary. From the time that a Black or Chicano or poor white is read his constitutional rights (rights he almost certainly does not comprehend or understand) by an arresting officer the chance of proving his innocence (if he is innocent) is remote. And that's precisely the task he faces—proving his innocence. For the reality of the American legal system is, despite lofty rhetoric to the contrary, that the state must do very little to establish the guilt of the disadvantaged man accused of committing a crime.

When a case is presented to the district attorney, the arresting officer's word is taken as truth. The accused is then hauled before a magistrate, who examines the evidence in the case, and almost always automatically sustains the charges, remanding the accused to jail and setting bail. The bail figure is usually too high for relatives and friends of a poor individual to raise. Consequently, the accused remains in jail until the day of the trial, which may not occur until six to thirty-six months from the time of arrest.

The accused languishes in jail during this period, despite the fact that under law, he is innocent until proven guilty. In the unlikely prospect that he is eventually cleared, he has still lost one, two, or three years out of his life. This is the reality for most persons of limited means who are accused of serious crimes under current criminal justice system.

Constitutional rights to remain silent, to be represented by competent legal counsel, to be tried by a jury of peers, are just so many meaningless verbal machinations. In the final analysis, a poor defendant knows that his silence will be regarded as self-incriminating, that his legal counsel will be ill-prepared or incompetent or at least without sufficient resources to prepare and present his case adequately, and that none of his peers will sit on the jury. He also knows he will be tried, convicted, and sentenced to death largely because of his economic or minority status—or both.

Lest someone misinterpret these remarks, they are not intended to infer that some Blacks or some Chicanos or some poor whites do not commit serious crimes. Of course they do, and those who are menaces to themselves and to society must be dealt with quickly, fairly, and with justice. But the government's own statistics reveal that these segments of society commit felonies at about the same ratio as all other elements, including the much larger white middle class. If the myth of America is to be maintained, dispensing punishment disproportionately, just because they are poor, Black, Chicano—or green-skinned Martian—must stop. It must stop now. Otherwise, our vaunted traditions of a free society, with justice towards all, are just so many meaningless words. And yet we see the highest court of the land affirm by a 5-4 margin, on April 22, 1987, that the death penalty is fair to minorities, despite the acknowledged fact that it kills many more of them than the mainstream of American society. *O tempora, o mores!*

If the rich do manage to escape the maximum penalty just because they can afford competent, experienced, well-paid legal counsel, what does this say about the inherent values of American society? What comment does this make on the American way of justice? Of Florida's 259 prisoners on death row, more than forty presently linger in the last stages of their cases wthout appropriate legal representation. State law guarantees the accused legal counsel only through the state Court of Appeals, plus a clemency hearing before the governor. Any appeals at higher levels are thereafter made at the prisoner's expense. Governor Robert Graham (now a U.S. senator) signed, while in office, all eighty warrants for execution, making the reality of applications for clemency or commutation of sentence utterly meaningless. Florida would do better to save its taxpayers money by declaring before each trial that any death sentence imposed is non-negotiable.

Unless a lawyer volunteers his services to represent the condemned after he has reached the appeals court level, the judicial process is abruptly halted. Most attorneys are simply not willing to volunteer $10,000-$20,000 in personal expenses for court records, witness interrogations, travel costs for expert witnesses, transcripts, not to mention the value of their own time, in order to represent an indigent felon before a federal court.

Mille Duvoric, a public defender for Montgomery County, Maryland, states that minimum cost of defending a person accused in a capital offense case is $156,000 in Maryland without any appellate review. She said that appellate costs in the state usually exceeded one-half million dollars. Who can afford such expensive legal costs? Surely those who have been convicted of murder and sentenced to die cannot, in the vast majority of cases.

Less than 1% of the over 2,000 inmates now sitting on death row had legal counsel paid for by private funds. Over 99% of those awaiting execution are indigents who were represented by public defenders or counsel appointed by the courts. This ratio of convicted indigents should not be viewed as a criticism of the competency or dedication of those noble young men and women working in public defenders' offices nationwide. The problem is much larger, the blame more widespread.

Many communities refuse to establish public defender organizations, therefore the judge is obliged to appoint counsel *pro bono*—without pay. And that's the crux of the problem. What attorney is going to spend weeks, months, and perhaps years pursuing a case without any compensation? How many attorneys could afford to? Large legal corporations are perhaps best-placed to perform such services, but tend to shy away from such nonprofitable work.

In many states, the maximum the state will pay for the felony case of an indigent is $1,000. In Georgia, no state funds are appropriated for legal defense of indigents. That responsibility is left up to the local communities. In 1982, the counties provided an average of only $131 in legal services for each indigent on trial. Georgia is the state that has only 100 convicted murderers awaiting execution. Only four other states (California, Florida, Illinois and Texas) have more awaiting execution than Georgia.

Unfortunately, there is no constitutional guarantee of competent legal counsel for the accused. The courts have held that everyone is entitled to counsel. The quality of that representation has never been addressed. Many on death row and many more serving life sentences in prison are the most visible victims of the failure to mandate competent counsel by simultaneously insuring adequate compensation for same.

Supreme Court Justice Thurgood Marshall has said:

> Often trial counsel simply are unfamiliar with the special rules that apply in capital cases....Thus, in cases I have read, counsel have been unaware that certain death penalty issues are pending before the appellate courts and pending that certain findings by a jury might preclude imposition of the death penalty....The federal reports are filled with stories of counsel who presented no evidence in mitigation of their client's sentences because they did not know what to offer or how to offer it, or had not read the state's sentencing statute.[46]

For ten years, the American Bar Association has attempted to rectify this injustice. In 1979, the ABA adopted a resolution urging the

U.S. Supreme Court "to adopt a rule providing for appointment of counsel to prepare petitions for discretioniary review of state court convictions of indigent death row inmates." The resolution also included an offer by the ABA to assist the Court in identifying qualified lawyers willing to accept appointments in such cases.

"The Supreme Court never responded to the resolution."[47]

Of course, some have argued that the accused has a right to defend himself. But most are unfamiliar wth the law, are unable to read at more than a fourth-grade level, and lack adequate command of the English language. Add to that predicament the fact that many correctional employees actively participate in harrassing those on death row. Law libraries are not properly stocked with law books. In Florida, the law library is not available to inmates without special permission. In some prisons, inmates with legal background are not permitted to assist others in the filing of briefs. When one analyzes these factors, one quickly understands that the average inmate's chances for the successful overturn of a conviction approach zero.

10. A DIS-UNITED FEDERATION OF STATES

The inequities of capital punishment in this country are not confined to race and class. One must also take into account the vagaries of state and local law, quirks which make the application of the penalty from jurisdiction to jurisdiction so vast as to be irreconcilable. Firstly, there is no uniformity among the states as to what crimes justify imposition of a death sentence. Secondly, there is no universal standard of execution for the same crimes. Thirdly, capital punishment is illegal in twelve of the fifty states. Fourthly, there is no assurance that all persons committing the same crime under the same circumstances in the same state (not to mention any other state) will receive the same punishment.

Among those states permitting capital punishment, a convicted felon may receive death in one instance, while another convicted of the same crime can escape with a lesser sentence, even when the two persons conspire to commit the same murder, and are tried and convicted jointly by the same jury.

Sentencing for crimes also differs substantially from state to state and even within the same state, depending on many diverse factors, including race, sex, and/or the financial status of the accused. Only 20% of women sentenced to death are actually executed, the sentences of the others usually being commuted to life in prison. Many women who commit capital crimes are not sentenced to death because predominantly male juries are reluctant to impose the death sentence on females.

Even more perplexing is the fact that a particular crime may be regarded as worthy of the death penalty in one state, and not in the other thirty-seven which use capital punishment. First degree murder, kidnapping, rape, arson-murder, aggravated carnal knowledge, robbery with intent to kill, treason, narcotics felonies, hijacking, and murder-for-hire may or may not be capital offenses, in different jurisdictions (see Table VIII-A in the Appendix). The same crime in another state may not be subject to the death penalty—for no apparent reason. The fact is, there are no local, regional, or national standards for determining when and under what circumstances criminals are or should be executed.

Despite the shortcomings of the judicial system, a majority of Americans blindly continue to support capital punishment. The FBI has released data on more than 17,000 homicides commtted in eight states, randomly selected over a five-year period. These show that only 2% of those committing murder in these states actually were given the death sentence, and that far fewer of them were actually executed. Still, most Americans would contend that capital punishment is imminently fair to all segments of society.

In practice and application, capital punishment is applied in such an arbitrary and discriminatory way in America that there is no defensible argument—moral, legal, or ethical—justifying its continued use.

11. GRAND JURIES OFFER NO PROTECTION

The original intent of the grand jury system was to protect the innocent from false accusations. Supposedly, a group of one's neighbors deliberating in secret would determine if sufficient evidence existed to bring criminal charges. They were designed to serve as a counterbalance to government abuses and excesses.

The idea was brought to this country from England, and was developed as an intricate and prudent body of law to balance the rights of individual freedom with the interest of the state in protecting society against criminals. However majestic the underlying principle of grand juries, their noble conceptions have been transformed into ignoble deceptions.

Fundamental interests of the individual are disregarded as prosecutors manipulate these panels for their own personal aggrandizement, using them as tools to harass, intimidate, and in some instances to frame those who are incapable of defending themselves.

Proceedings of grand juries are secret only as they relate to the defendant. It is a common practice for some prosecutors to anonymously leak damaging, derogatory, or unsubstantiated testimony regarding the accused, thus discrediting him to such an extent that he can never legally recover. In this post-Watergate era, the irresponsible style of investigative reporting, using leaked testimony to overdramatize serious allegations of criminal behavior, often renders a grand jury indictment synonymous with guilt.

The accused is not permitted legal counsel when appearing before a grand jury, while the prosecutor comes armed with his many legal talents. The accused is not afforded the basic right of being confronted by his accusers, who in some instances are anonymous or even nonexistent, nor is he allowed to cross examine those who make the charges.

Indictments are frequently written by the prosecutor, independent of consultation with the grand jurors, and then automatically (and sometimes unwittingly) approved without serious study. In effect, many grand juries are little more than rubber stamps in the hands of aggressive district attorneys.

In the present climate of hysteria about crime, "innocent until proven guilty" is often a rhetorical fantasy. Indictment is usually automatic after accusations have been widely publicized by the media. This procedure has become a standard charade, placing the onus of guilt on the accused, and forcing him, in effect, to prove his innocence in a public forum. And it is a truism that no matter how much any individual protests his or her innocence to the media, there will always be a certain measure of mud that will continue to cling to that person for the rest of his or her professional and personal life.

12. THE INCONSISTENCY OF OUR JUDGES

The ultimate responsibility for the accelerated resumption of executions in this country lies, of course, with state and local judges. The arrogance of power often displayed by them is based on a presumption that only judges should be allowed to make life and death decisions. Many judges labor under the impression that they are pontifically annointed, instead of politically appointed.

Some have even expressed frustration at the fact that juries can challenge their perceived authority in this area, holding that ordinary citizens can not be entrusted with such momentous decisions. Consequently, some judges consistently overrule jury verdicts of life in prison to impose a death sentence. A jury that hears the same case, analyzes the same set of circumstances, evaluates the same facts as a judge, and recommends life instead of death is sometimes described by conservatives as "soft on crime."

If judges are to be consistent in their deliberations, they must consider all sides of the issue. Those judges who contend that they have the right to take cases away from juries for the purpose of imposing a death sentence must also recognize the fact that they have an equal obligation to remove cases from juries for the purpose of sparing the lives of innocent or falsely-accused persons. In too many instances, weak judges have permitted persons to be sentenced to death where the evidence simply does not support such a verdict. Supreme Court Justice Felix Frankfurter has said:

> The easy but timid way out for a trial judge is to leave all cases tried to a jury determination, but in so doing, he fails in his duty to take a case from the jury when the evidence would not warrant a verdict by it. A *timid judge*, like a biased judge, is intrinsically a *lawless judge*. [Emphasis added, and the case did not involve the death penalty.][48]

Most supporters of capital punishment deny that innocent persons often are executed. But facts are not on their side. The *Stanford Law Review* conducted a detailed, comprehensive study of the innocent who have been executed. The research was conducted by Hugo Bedau of Tufts University and Michael Radelet of the University of Florida. They reported that 350 men sentenced to death were later proven to be innocent. Twenty-three of them were actually executed. The true figure must be much higher, since 350 reflects only those cases where the real murderer confessed or the state eventually admitted a mistake.

According to some judges, capital punishment should be the exclusive prerogative of those who have distinguished themselves by graduating from accredited schools of law and who have either ingratiated themselves with politicians to secure their original appointments to the bench, or have taken popular stands on issues like the death penalty to ensure their elections and re-elections. They often reflect a cavalier attitude that includes an obsession for brutal treatment. Typical is the attitude expressed by the judge in South Carolina who sentenced fourteen-year-old

George Stinney to the electric chair on June 16, 1944. The judge's attitude was: "If he's old enough to commit the crime, then he's old enough to pay for it." Even more terrifying was the response from one of the jurors:

> I wouldn't want to torture the boy. But I think if you can get him out of the world as humanely as possible—show a little more humanity than he did—well, get him out.[49]

It is an ironic perversity that some judges who routinely sentence felons to death also issue restraining orders to prevent others from taking their own lives. Elizabeth Bouvia, a 26-year-old quadriplegic, wished to starve herself to death rather than suffer severe pain. She was prevented from doing so by an injunction forbidding her from committing suicide, and prohibiting hospital personnel, friends, or relatives from offering assistance. Hospital personnel force-fed her daily, therefore violating what little dignity she had left.

Without condoning suicide or euthanasia, the question should still be asked: when is it proper for a handful of officials in positions of power to reserve for themselves the right to decide when, where, how, and who shall die? A judge who sees no contradiction, feels no compunction, loses no sleep, after condemning one human to death, yet discerns a fine line of morality when another person assumes that same right for herself, is indeed tampering with the powers of deity. While the judge in this particular case may never have sentenced a person to death, many judges who have done so would have ruled in precisely the same way. What divine *fiat* gives judges the right to ignore the wishes of one individual in a free society to take her own life (for whatever reason), and at the same time personally to assume the power to take another individual's life (for whatever reason). Have we become so self-righteous? Will judges now declare *ex cathedra* their own infallibility? I personally would not be surprised by such *hubris*.

13. DISCRETIONARY SENTENCING PRACTICES

The Supreme Court, in an attempt to establish some standard for imposing the death penalty, has outlined a procedure to be followed. Conceptually, it guarantees fairness in dispensing the sentence and dispels the contention that capital punishment is arbitrary and capricious.

Under these guidelines, sufficient notice in advance of a trial that the prosecutor will seek the death penalty is required. The accused must be represented by competent legal counsel. If convicted, a post-verdict sentence hearing is mandated where the government may present evidence of aggravating circumstances, and the defendant may present such mitigating factors as he or his counsel deems pertinent. The matter is then deliberated to determine if the aggravating factors outweigh the mitigating ones. By unanimous agreement a decision must be reached. But under no circumstance can a jury consider race, color, national origin, creed, or sex in deciding the verdict.

The procedure is high-sounding rhetoric, purporting to protect the rights of the accused. But it is laden with flaws and fallacies. In the first place, 90% of those sentenced to die do not have "competent legal counsel." They are wards of the state and appointed representation by the courts. Usually, they are defended by attorneys who have no prior experience in criminal cases and most certainly none in capital offense cases. In the second place, how would the penniless defendant pay for the necessary investigation to secure additional mitigating evidence? Testimony from psychiatric, sociological, and psychological experts does not come cheap. Thirdly, everybody sitting on the judgment panel has already sworn his or her belief in capital punishment as just retribution for convicted murderers.

One of the most serious problems facing our system of criminal justice is the wide discretion allowed juries and judges in the sentencing process. The basic question is not the right of judges and juries to impose punishment—that's their responsibility under the law. Rather, the issue is their inability or refusal to discharge this responsibility in the same fashion for all classes of people and for all similar crimes. Murder is murder, the wanton taking of human life. First-degree murder is the unlawful killing of another human with premeditated malice. Grading it into different categories and assessing penalties in differing degrees depending upon the self-perceived seriousness of the crime is ludicrous. It's a judicial hoax which establishes an escape hatch for those with political or community clout. Allowing juries and judges to consider such extenuating circumstances as motivation, status, or even race guarantees that capital punishment in most instances will be arbitrarily and capriciously applied.

The variety of ways in which individual states rewrote their laws after the *Furman* case to allow for differing types of discretion in imposing the death sentence, shows that for all practical purposes, the Supreme

Court ruling against "arbitrary and capricious" sentencing has no relevancy. Even within the confines of one state there can be a vast disparity in how murder cases are handled and resolved. Some local prosecutors automatically seek death in every first-degree murder case. Others just a few miles distant may never ask for it.

What appears to be an extra safeguard against willy-nilly imposition of the death penalty, the requirement that a jury first establish guilt, and then in a separate action determine punishment, is just another part of the charade. Until the courts have clearly established the right of those who disagree with capital punishment to sit on juries in capital offense cases, the verdict of death will continue to be haphazard and automatic.

The case of Doyle Skillern, convicted as an accomplice to a Texas murder, is a perfect example of the mischievous latitude allowed juries in sentencing. Skillern waited outside while his partner in crime shot a Texas undercover narcotics agent to death. For his role in driving the getaway car, he was executed. The killer was given life in prison. The *Saint Louis Post-Dispatch* commented editorially:

> When the Supreme Court reinstated the death penalty in 1976, it intended that the ultimate punishment should not be ordained, as it has been, in a "wanton and freakish" manner. Which brings us to Doyle Skillern's accomplice, Charles Sanne, the killer. What punishment did Texas decree for him? As it turned out, the jury decided that Sanne provided no continuing threat to society. He was given a life sentence. Indeed, the man who pulled the trigger and fired six shots into the body of the narcotics agent is even now being considered for parole.[50]

More disheartening than such indiscriminate sentencing to death and the carefree manner with which it has been applied, is the institutionalized bias against a convicted murderer. Our judicial system has as its bedrock a fetishness for procedure. At the appellate level, only procedural error is permitted. Jurists don't want to be bothered with the merits or demerits of the case. Their sole concern is that legal procedure was observed meticulously. The situation is utterly absurd: even if constitutional error is established at the appeals court level, if the defense attorney has failed to object at the time of the initial trial, the error is not admissible on appeal.

Most poor people charged with capital offenses are convicted; more than a fair percentage are executed. The wealthy and influential are able to maneuver through a maze of legal protections in avoiding the death sentence. Sloppy investigations at the beginning, sympathetic prosecutors, plea bargaining, *nolo* processes, *nolo contendere*, reduced sentences, early parole—these are the resources that wealthier individuals can count on for vindication. Common folk lacking such resources become the victims sitting on our death rows.

The unfairness of the whole process shows itself in the fact that wealthy persons who commit murder invariably are charged with manslaughter (a lesser offense), while the very poor invariably are accused of first-degree murder (a much more serious charge). Crimes committed by the poor are called "heinous," those perpetrated by white collar types as "ungentlemanly indiscretions." But justice, if it is to be regarded as "just" by the great mass of Americans, cannot engage in such frivolous distinctions. Reverence for life styles, not respect for life, is now the most important criterion for unfairly adjudicating punishment in our modern system of values.

14. THE VICTIMS' RIGHTS MOVEMENT

The right of victims to be heard in court has emerged as a new phenomenon in the legal system. "Victim" is not limited to the one personally abused, but also includes any relative, friend, or neighbor who feels aggrieved by a criminal assault on someone else. Those pronouncing sentence are permitted to take into account the amount of harm or damage caused to third-party, innocent persons. They are allowed to testify even if they are not eyewitnesses. Proponents argue that these rights should apply in all criminal cases. Again, the fate of the accused may depend on how a particular jurisdiction handles these cases—and the public clamor they generate.

The idea of "victim" input into criminal proceedings is a novel, even radical concept. Until very recently, trial proceedings have been adversarial, at least in the sense that the prosecutor protected the rights of the state (or victim), and the defense counsel the rights of the defendant. The judge and jury supposedly have acted as impartial arbiters in the contest. The prosecutor was heard, the defense was heard, the accused even had the right to be heard. But the victim's wife, children, mother, or neighbors did not enjoy the same privilege, unless they were witnesses to the crime.

To Kill or Not to Kill

When New York Republican Congressman Hamilton Fish was mugged on Capitol Hill, he started a citizens' anti-crime group, the National Victims of Crime. It now has over 50,000 members.

Since then, many other groups have sprung up around the country demanding the same rights. The mother of a twenty-two-year-old girl who was raped and murdered was permitted to testify in a recent Maryland criminal trial. If any felon has ever deserved the death penalty, certainly this one did. According to John Sansing:

> The world of Roberta and Vincent Roper was shattered last April 3. The couple lived with their five children in a house they had built on several acres of land outside Upper Marlboro in Prince George's County, Maryland. Their daughter, Stephanie, the oldest and, according to her mother, the role model for her four younger siblings, disappeared that night on her way home from an evening in Washington, D.C. Several days later her body was found: she had been raped repeatedly, beaten with a logging chain, shot in the forehead, drenched wth gasoline and set on fire, and dumped in six inches of water in the Patuxent River.
>
> The last hours of her daughter's life play in Roberta Roper's mind like a continuous videotape. "It's only recently," she says, "that I've been able to remember the joyful times. Only now are those times not completely pushed out by the horror of that night."
>
> Two men were quickly apprehended: Jack Ronald Jones, 26, and Jerry Lee Beatty. Jones was tagged as the leader, Beatty the follower. There was never much doubt about their guilt. Legal confessions were obtained, and the prime issue at Jones's trial was whether he would get the death sentence.
>
> A group of friends rallied around the Ropers and became a commanding presence at all hearings; at one point a defense lawyer was reported to have branded the group "a lynch mob." Mrs. Roper attended all the hearings she could, but resolved to talk only of the life of Stephanie, and not of the defendants or the proceedings. She says she began with a faith in the process, including a belief that adequate punishment would be meted out. "You would like to feel that the killer of

your child is going to be punished."

Beatty testified and worked out a plea arrangement with the state attorney's office. After Jones' guilt was established, evidence and argument were heard on whether he should be put to death. The jury in Baltimore County, Maryland—to which the trial had been transferred because of wide publicity in the Washington area—said no.

Fifteen minutes later, Circuit Judge Walter R. Haile sentenced Jones to life imprisonment for murder, life imprisonment for rape, and twenty years for kidnapping. However, because Haile gave concurrent rather than consecutive sentences, Jones is serving each sentence at the same time; thus, he is eligible for parole in about twelve years.[51]

The *Roper* case involves all the controversial issues surrounding the debate on capital punishment, and has been used as an example both by those who advocate the death penalty and by those who oppose it. Unquestionably, the crime was heinous, unprovoked, gruesome. There is no doubt whatever about the guilt of the accused and the innocence of the victim. Most fair-minded persons would agree that in this case the punishment was too lenient.

On the other hand, those opposed to capital punishment can readily provide a laundry list of inconsistencies in the proceedings which support their position. Without attempting to justify the sentence imposed, they point out flagrant flaws in the process. Firstly, they argue that this case was so well-publicized that in order for the accused to receive a fair trial, the trial should have been held at another jurisdiction. Secondly, the allowance of "plea bargaining" by one criminal to assure the conviction of another underminded the legal concept of equal treatment and equal punishment for the same crimes. Thirdly, a jury of one's peers rejected the prosecution's request for the death penalty; those who support the death penalty should now abide by the jury's decision. Fourthly, the judge's discretionary changes in the sentence further document the contention that only the disadvantaged who are found guilty of heinous crimes receive the death penalty.

Because the law makes the criminal in such cases eligible for parole after twelve years, no one can foresee how long Jack R. Jones will actually spend in prison—or when he will again be free to menace the

Stephanie Ropers of this world.

The irony of the whole situation is that Roberta Roper, mother of the slain woman, was only seeking some appropriate punishment for the villains. She has publicly declared her opposition to capital punishment—even in this case.

Thirty-six states enacted laws requiring that victim impact statements be filed at the time of sentencing, detailing the misery the defendant inflicted on relatives and friends of the victim. Maryland passed such a law in 1983, which was later challenged as unconstitutional. The Maryland Court of Appeals (*Booth v.Maryland*) upheld its legality in 1986. On June 15, 1987, the U.S. Supreme Court in a 5-4 decision ruled that the use of impact statements in sentencing violated the Eighth Amendment rights against "cruel and unusual" punishment. Justice Lewis Powell, in delivering the opinion of the Court, said:

> One can understand the grief and anger of the family caused by the brutal murders in this case, and there is no doubt that jurors generally are aware of these feelings. But the formal presentation of this information by the state can serve no other purpose than to inflame the jury and divert it from deciding the case on the relevant evidence concerning the crime and defendant. As we have noted, any decision to impose the death sentence must "be, and appear to be, based on reason rather than caprice or emotion."[52]

15. YOUTH AND THE DEATH PENALTY

Even most advocates of the death penalty argue that young people should be exempted. Many Americans undoubtedly believe that our youth already enjoy that status. Such, however, is not the case. In the same haphazard and inconsistent way that the death penalty has been applied to adults, so has it also been used to execute juveniles in some states. Since 1900, almost two hundred minors have been executed.

The following article by Ruth Simon documents the situation in minute detail:

25 JUVENILES ON DEATH ROW;
SHOULD AGE BARRIERS BE SET?

As many as 25 of the nation's death row inmates were juveniles at the time their crimes were committed—a fact that is prompting a reexamination of whether juveniles should ever be sentenced to death.

Thirty of the 38 states that permit capital punishment allow criminals to be executed regardless of their age, and the nation's death row population includes between 20 and 25 juvenile offenders, according to Victor L. Streib, associate dean of the Cleveland-Marshall College of Law, and an authority on the death penalty for juveniles.

The American Bar Association will take up the question of capital punishment for juveniles this week when it considers a proposal opposing their execution. The issue raises questions concerning the purpose of capital punishment, as well as the age at which individuals can be held responsible for their actions. A juvenile is generally defined as someone under the ages of 16 or 18, depending on the state.

Although the majority of nations have set 18 as the minimum age for capital punishment, 288 juveniles have been executed in the United States under laws that permit certain young offenders to be tried as adults, according to Mr. Streib.

The last such execution came in 1964, when the state of Texas electrocuted James Echols, who was convicted of a rape committed when he was 17 [*Echols v. State*, 370 S.W. 2d 892 (1963)]. The largest number of executions have occurred in Georgia, which has permitted 40 condemned juveniles to die; the youngest person executed in this century was a 13-year-old in Florida who was put to death in 1927.

Under current law, judges must expressly consider the age of an offender before imposing the death penalty. The defendant's age, however, may be outweighed by other aggravating factors.

Opponents of this process argue that the execution of any juvenile constitutes "cruel and unusual punishment" in violation of the Eighth Amendment. "There's a continuing sense that a child's behavior is different from an adult's behavior," said Mr. Streib.

Some observers have also extended this analysis to individuals who have the mental age of a juvenile and the chronological age of an adult. "If they're not mentally adults...I just wonder if the same standard of law would be applied," said Watt Espy of the University of Alabama Law Center's Capital Punishment Project.

Supporters of the death penalty, on the other hand, suggest that youthful offenders should not be permitted to "wrap themselves in the shield of...age" in order to escape responsibility for their crimes.

"In many cases they fully understand their actions," said Nicholas Calio of the Washington Legal Foundation, a Washington, D.C.-based conservative public-interest legal group. (NLJ, May 23.) The rationale for imposing the death penalty is "in some cases stronger" when a juvenile is involved, he added.

The U.S. Supreme Court bypassed an opportunity to evaluate these conflicting arguments last year when it ruled on an appeal filed by Monty Lee Eddings, who was convicted of killing a police officer when he was 16. Instead of ruling on the constitutionality of the death penalty for juveniles, as most observers expected, the court chose to remand the case to the Oklahoma Court of Criminal Appeals for further consideration of "mitigating factors" [*Eddings v. Oklahoma*, 455 U.S. 104 (1982)].[53]

—Ruth Simon

Two scores of young men solemnly await the day officials wll lead them down the corridors of state prisons to die. Many of them were only fifteen when convicted of capital murder.

Like those persons who have been sentenced to death for crimes committed before they were eighteen years of age, they nervously read all publications dealing with the legality of executing minors. State laws concerning age and executions vary. Minimum ages ranging from ten years to eighteen years for executions exist in twenty-three states. Fourteen states and the federal government have no specific minimum age (see Table VIII in the Appendix).

On January 10, 1986, James Terry Roach was executed in a South Carolina prison. He was seventeen when accused and convicted of murdering two other teenagers (ages fourteen and fifteen). Was he an incorrigible, habitual criminal? No! Prior to this incident, his only previous involvement wth the law was a minor infraction for taking his father's car without permission. His I.Q. was measured at 68, close to the mental retardation level. Compounding the situation is the fact that he was suffering from Huntington's Chorea, an incurable neurological disease, at the time of his execution.

If any case ever justified commutation of a sentence to life in prison, this was one. Perhaps the governor of South Carolina failed to ask himself the same question as Samuel F. B. Morse, who cited a quote from the Book of Numbers in the Bible when he said, "What hath God wrought?"[54]

16. THE SECRET DOSSIER ON YOUTH EXECUTIONS

The best kept secret in America is the number of young people who have been executed in the United States. In only twenty-three states is the age of the offender considered in applying the death sentence, and even here the limits are often set ridiculously low (age ten, for example). The others have no laws, rules, or tradition for mitigation in the execution of those under age eighteen. Maryland's highest court ruled in 1984 that teenagers were not exempt from capital punishment laws. The judge ruled that the accused, who was convicted of bashing in the head of the victim with a baseball bat, repeatedly raping her, and then slitting her throat, was not exercising a usual teenage prank. He described it as a cold brutal act of repeated sadistic violence. Of course it was. However, only the act of violence itself was a consideration. Court testimony in the case shows that the youth (who pleaded not guilty because of insanity) had a measured I.Q. of 64, defined as imbecile level or borderline retardation by psychiatric experts.

Since the government started compiling records of capital punishment, 288 juveniles have been executed. Twenty-nine states permit them to be tried as adults in certain cases and under certain circumstances, and treated in such instances as adults. Forty juveniles in this century have been executed in the sovereign state of Georgia. Florida, the Sunshine State and home of Disney World, executed a thirteen-year-old child in 1927. But the federal government has engaged in an even more dastardly act by executing a young man who committed a crime at the age of ten! In 1885, the federal government executed a Cherokee Indian lad by the name of James Arcene who was twenty-two years of age. After the commission of the crime, at which time Arcene was ten years of age, he escaped, only to be arrested eleven years later.

A divided Supreme Court in June 1988 struck down as unconstitutional those laws in eighteen states which allowed execution of persons who were under sixteen years of age when they committed a capital crime. But the majority opinion left open the possibility of state legislatures enacting laws which specifically authorize the executions of juveniles.

What does this mean in a civilized society? Thirty-five youths are now awaiting execution in the thirty-eight states that permit capital punishment. In the history of Florida, four youths aged sixteen have been electrocuted, four aged seventeen, one aged fourteen, and *one aged thirteen*. All of them suffered the prescribed penalties for violating the law. Did they understand why they had to pay the ultimate price for their crimes? Does a thirteen-year-old have any concept of premeditated murder?

This nation, collectively and individually, must arrive at a sensible, fair, humane definiton of the purpose of punishment. Discipline, if excessive or brutal, loses its impact. Reverend George Lundy, S.J., director of the Institute of Human Relations at Loyola University in New Orleans, says that punishment should accomplish four ends: restore what was lost to the victim, provide rehabilitation, apply equally to all classes of people, and be no harsher than necessary.

Assessment of the death penalty convinces many that it lacks all four qualities: death cannot restore life to the victim; it cannot rehabilitate the villain; it does not apply to all classes equally; and it is the harshest of all human punishments.

Perpetrators of violent crime, of whatever age or sex or race, must be caught, tried, and justly punished. Putting thirteen- and fourteen-year-olds to death should give any reasonable person reason to pause in sober deliberation. A person too young to enter into a legal contract, too young legally to engage in sex, too young to vote, too young even to purchase alcoholic spirits, too young to enlist in the military, should also be too young to be executed.

17. MISTAKEN IDENTITY

The ultimate inequity of the criminal system is the execution of the innocent. While it seems certain that such catastrophies are not an everyday occurrence, they have happened and will continue to happen. Murder by the state of even one innocent victim must surely be an outrage to even the most steadfast advocate of the death penalty.

Despite the fact that more than one-third of all death penalty cases heard by the 11th U.S. Circuit Court of Appeals (Florida, Georgia, and Alabama) have been overturned in recent years, these states continue to impose capital punishment.

There is no shortage of cases where the guilt of those condemned to die was less than certain. Pope John Paul II personally intervened in a Florida case by making a last-minute telephone call to Florida Governor Robert Graham, pleading that the life of Robert Sullivan be spared. Sullivan had been convicted of killing the night manager of a Howard Johnson's restaurant, and spent more than ten years on death row. He was finally electrocuted (despite the Pope's intervention) on November 30, 1983.

According to one story which appeared in the *Florida Times Union*, Sullivan stated that he was in a Miami gay bar at the time of the murder. Catholic Bishop John H. Snyder told the same newspaper that a Boston man had confessed to his priest that he was with Sullivan in the same establishment at the time at which the crime reportedly took place; but Snyder was unable to provide further information about the witness because revealing details given in the confessional is automatic grounds for excommunication from the Church.

Reportedly, the individual would not testify on behalf of Sullivan because his family did not know about his homosexuality. The Sullivan execution is a classic example of why the death penalty should be abolished. It involved: circumstantial evidence, denial of guilt, uncertainty of state witnesses. Yet, because a governor refused to rescind the order, the execution went forward.

Governor Graham, now a U.S. senator, was not a person disposed to showing leniency to convicted criminals, no matter what extenuating evidence was produced. In a later press conference which was not specifically related to the *Sullivan* case, but which touched generally on the commutation of death sentences, the governor said, "I do not consider carrying out a duty which is mine to be inconsistent with Christian values."[55]

This attitude of responsible individuals dodging individual responsibilities is all too reminiscent of the indefensible defense offered by war criminals at Nürnberg, who were only "carrying out orders."

The *Sullivan* case illustrates the irrationalities and inconsistencies of the criminal justice system. A friend of Sullivan's, Reid McClaughlin, was allegedly an accomplice with Sullivan in the killing of the restaurant manager. McClaughlin testified for the state against Sullivan, receiving a life sentence, and was paroled in 1981. On the same day that one supposed perpetrator of a heinous crime, Robert Sullivan, was executed, another culprit in the same act, Reid McClaughlin, was walking the streets of Florida, a free man on parole.

An unfortunate example of mistaken identity was discussed in a recent *Washington Post* editorial:

> Ten years ago this week, William Velten was murdered and left in a ditch near Alburquerque, N.M. He had been castrated, slashed repeatedly wth a knife, and shot five times. The state pathologist said the victim had been sodomized and that the cuts had been made with a heated knife. A woman testified at the trial that she had been forced by the killers to watch this torture and murder, after which she was raped and slashed with the same hot knife. Four members of a motorcycle gang were convicted of the crimes and sentenced to die. They deserved it, right? Only one problem: after they spent 18 months on death row, it was discovered that the witness had lied. Someone else later confessed and was convicted of the murder.[56]

A classic example of an execution of an innocent person is the 1915 lynching of Leo Frank, a Jewish businessman in Atlanta, Georgia. If any case documents the inequity of treatment in the legal system of racial, political, or religious minorities, plus the insanity of mob rule, it is this particular miscarriage of justice.

Frank, the owner of a small factory which manufactured pencils, was falsely accused of murdering a 13-year-old girl whose badly beaten and strangled body was discovered in the basement of Frank's shop. Despite his protestations of innocence, a jury convicted him and sentenced him to death. During the trial, hundreds of demonstrators stood outside the court room chanting "hang the Jew" and similar racial epithets. After the judge had announced the death sentence and set a date for Frank's execution, a mob led by officials of the Ku Klux Klan stormed the prison in Milledgeville, Georgia, abducted Frank, and lynched him, on August 17, 1915.

But in 1982, Alonzo Mann, a young office boy in the plant at the time of the murder, came forward and admitted that he had seen a man other than Leo Frank carry the body of the girl into the basement. He feared for his life because of the hysteria surrounding the case, and withheld the information for sixty-seven years. On March 10, 1986, the Georgia Board of Pardons and Paroles granted posthumously a petition completely exonerating Leo Frank.

History is filled with similar examples of innocent people mistakenly identified and executed. However, some have been more fortunate than others. They have been accused, tried, convicted and cheated the gallows in the nick of time. There are enough cases where this has happened to give even the reddest of rednecks pause. Earl Charles, after two years on death row, was released because it was proven that he was not in the state at the time of the crime. Jerry Banks endured five years of torture on Geogia's death row before his innocence was established.

These examples merely scratch the surface in demonstrating the kinds of mistakes to which any criminal justice system is prone. The death penalty infinitely compounds these inevitable mistakes. Pardoning Leo Frank was little solace to his living relatives, and absolutely none at all to Frank himself. The state can release and recompense a man falsely imprisoned; only God can recompense the dead.

Americans would be within the bounds of profound reason and basic humanitarian values if they followed the dictates of Thomas Jefferson, who said:

> I shall ask for the abolition of the punishment of death until the infallibility of human judgment is demonstrated to me.[57]

On another occasion the author of the Declaration of Independence empathically stated:

> The care of human life and happiness, and not their destruction, is the first and only legitimate object of good government.[58]

It is my own opinion that a judge, a prosecutor, or twelve jurors who engage in deliberate, calculated procedures designed to take the life of another, are as guilty of premeditated murder as the criminal himself. If we are truly to regard ourselves as a civilized people, we must end this cycle of violence by following the lead of other civilized nations. Rehabilitate the criminal, if possible. If that is **not possible**, at least remove him from society so that he can do no further harm, either to himself or to others. A true Christian heritage of love, as stated in both the Old and New Testaments, is based on God's admonition, "Thou shalt not kill," and on Christ's gentle reminder to "Love one another." Neither statement mentions any exceptions.

Christians must set the example for the barbarians among us, for those who cry out for vengeance, for those who revel in war and death and bloody violence. We are a better people than that. Let us now go forward to abolish the stain of state-sponsored death. There are bigger, better challenges which we must meet, including the conquering of hunger, pollution, even the survival of mankind itself, and we had better turn our attention to these matters soon, before it is too late. Our society must affirm life, not glorify death. Let us choose, for perfectly sound and sane and moral reasons, not to kill, ever again.

NOTES

CHAPTER I

1. Anonymous. Prayer used by Alcoholics Anonymous groups.
2. Chavez, Rev. Guillermo, speaking before the House Committee on the Judiciary, Subcommittee on Criminal Justice, Nov. 7, 1985, p. 23.
3. *John* 10:10, *The Holy Bible*, edited by Rev. John P. O'Connell (Chicago: The Catholic Press Inc., 1950). Also: *Leviticus* 24:19-20, p. 105.
4. *Ibid., Book of Romans* 12:17-21.
5. Blank, Rabbi Irvin M., speaking before the House Committee on the Judiciary, Subcommittee on Criminal Justice, Nov. 7, 1985.
6. Goodman, Walter, quoting Bishop Renee Gracida of Corpus Christi, Texas, "Religious Alliance Against Executions Grows," in *The New York Times* (Dec. 7, 1983): B8.
7. General Conference, Mennonite Church, Estes Park, CO, July 16, 1985.
8. *Op. cit., The New York Times.*
9. *Ibid.*
10. *Ibid.*
11. *Ibid.*
12. *Ibid.*
13. 197th General Assembly Presbyterian Church (USA), June, 1985.
14. Rev. Chavez, Congressional Hearings, Nov. 7, 1985, p. 27.
15. Drinan, Robert E., "The Catholic Bishops of United States Oppose Capital Punishment," in *The Congressional Record* (Nov. 19, 1980): 3, E 5013.
16. *Ibid.*
17. *Ibid.*
18. "American Catholic Bishops Detail Opposition to Capital Punishment," in *The Washington Post* (Nov. 14, 1983): C5.
19. September 18, 1981 letter to Senator Strom Thurmond, in *The Congressional Record* (Aug. 14, 1983): S. 11843.
20. Gekas, George (R-Pa.), "Dear Colleague Letter," dated June 10, 1985.
21. "Antiabortionists Oppose Adding Other Causes to Pro-Life Banner," in *The Washington Post* (Jan. 30, 1984): 8.
22 "The Pope and the Death Penalty," in *Newsweek* (Dec. 12, 1983): 77.
23. Pope John Paul II, quoted in the *Washington Post* (Jan. 16, 1983).
24. *Op. cit., Newsweek.*
25. *Ibid.*
26. *Ibid.*
27. *Ibid.*
28. "Catholics Split on Life Issues," in *St. Louis Post-Dispatch* (Mar. 17, 1984): 60.
29. *Ibid*
30. Gross, Helg Bergold, source unknown.
31. Camus, Albert, "Reflections on the Guillotine," in *Evergreen Review* (1957).
32. *Exodus* 16-21, The Bible.

33.   *Ibid.*, 22-24.
34.   *Ibid.*, *Genesis* 50:19-21.
35.   *Ibid.*, *Genesis* 4:9, p. 4.
36.   *Ibid.*, *Genesis* 4:12-15.
37.   *Ibid.*, *Matthew* 5:38-41.
38.   *Ibid.*, *Proverbs* 25:2.
39.   *Talmud*, Makkot, Chapter 1; Misnah, p. 7.

CHAPTER II

1.   Thucydides, *Peloponnesian War*, 427 B.C.
2.   Brasfield, Philip, with Jeffrey M. Elliot. *Deathman Pass Me By: Two Years on Death Row* (San Bernardino, CA: The Borgo Press, 1983), p. 81.
3.   Mathews, Jay, in *The Washington Post* (Jan. 18, 1986): A3.
4.   *New York Times* (June 4, 1983).
5.   "An Eye for an Eye," in *Time* (Jan. 24, 1983): 6.
6.   "Sikeston Inquiry Seeks to Identify Men in Lynching," in *St. Louis Post-Dispatch* (Jan. 30, 1942): 3A.
7.   *Ibid.*
8.   "No Indictment for Lynching of Sikeston Negro," in *St. Louis Post-Dispatch* (Mar. 11, 1942): 3A
9.   "Sikeston Inquiry Seeks to Identify Men in Lynching," in *St. Louis Post-Dispatch* (Jan. 30, 1942): 3A
10.   Bedau, Hugo Adam. *The Case Against the Death Penalty* (New York: American Civil Liberties Union, 1984), p. 21.
11.   *Leviticus* 24:19-20, in *The Holy Bible*, edited by Rev. John O'Connelll (Chicago: The Catholic Press Inc., 1950), p. 105.
12.   Ibid., *Genesis* 9:6-7.
13.   Ibid., *Ezechiel* 33:10-11, p. 772.

CHAPTER III

1.   *Matthew* 21-23, *The Holy Bible*, p. 29.
2.   *Ibid.*, 21-23.
3.   *Ibid.*, 5:44-45.
4.   *Ibid.*, 5:20.
5.   *Judith* 8:15, The Bible.
6.   "An Eye for an Eye," in *Time* (Jan. 14, 1983): 6.
7.   *Luke* 23:34, *The Holy Bible*.
8.   *John* 8:7, *Ibid.*
9.   *Ibid.*, *Book of Numbers* 35:30, p. 145.
10.   Craveri, Marcello, *The Life of Jesus* (New York: Echo Press, 1989).
11.   *Matthew* 52-53, *The Holy Bible*, p. 28.
12.   Jefferson, Thomas, Declaration of Independence, July 5, 1776.
13.   *Time* (Jan. 24, 1983): 36.
14.   Dante Alighieri, *Inferno*, Canto III, line 32.

CHAPTER IV

1. Bedau, Hugo, *The Death Penalty in America* (Garden City, NY: Anchor Books, 1964), p. 260.

2. Knorr, Stephen J., "Deterrence and the Death Penalty: A Temporal Cross-Sectional Approach," in *Journal of Criminal Law and Criminology* 70 (Summer, 1979): 236.

3. Berns, Walter, *For Capital Punishment* (New York: Basic Books, 1979), p. 104-5.

4. Scheussler, Karl F., "The Deterrent Influence of the Death Penalty," in *The Annals* 284 (Nov., 1952): 57.

5. Bedau, p. 262.

6. Sellin, Thorsten, *The Death Penalty* (Philadelphia: American Law Institute, 1959), p. 34. Sellin later extended the comparison through 1963 in his *Capital Punishment* (New York: Harper & Row, 1967, p. 138), and reached the same conclusion.

7. Scheussler, p. 58; Chambliss, W., "Types of Deviance and the Effectiveness of Legal Sanctions," in *Wisconsin Law Review* (Summer, 1967): 703.

8. Ehrlich, Isaac, "Deterrence: Evidence and Inferrence," in *Yale Law Journal* 85 (Dec., 1975): 222-23.

9. Peck, Jon K., "The Deterrent Effect of Capital Punishment: Ehrlich and His Critics," in *Yale Law Journal* 85 (Jan., 1976): 364.

10. Van den Haag, Ernest, "On Deterrence and the Death Penalty," in *Journal of Criminal Law, Criminology and Police Science* 60 (June, 1969): 145-46.

11. Peck, p. 364; Ehrlich, Isaac, "The Deterrent Effect of Capital Punishment: A Question of Life and Death," in *American Economic Review* 65 (June, 1975): 415.

12. Sellin, p. 124.

13. Ehrlich, "Deterrent Effect of Capital Punishment," p. 397-417.

14. *Ibid.*, p. 414.

15. Klein, Lawrence R., Brian Forst, and Victor Filatov, "The Deterrent Effect of Capital Punishment: An Assessment of the Estimates," in Blumstein, Alfred, Jacqueline Cohen, and Daniel Nagel, eds., *Deterrence and Incapacitation: Estimating the Effects of Criminal Sanctions on Crime Rates* (Washington: National Academy of Sciences, 1978), p. 345.

16. Baldus, David C., and James W. L. Cole, "A Comparison of the Work of Thorsten Sellin and Isaac Ehrlich on the Deterrent Effect of Capital Punishment," in *Yale Law Journal* 85 (Dec., 1975): 170.

17. A summary of the criticism of Ehrlich's work is found in Klein, Lawrence R., Brian Forst, and Victor Filatov, "The Deterrent Effect of Capital Punishment," p. 336-360.

18. McGahey, Richard M., "Economic Theory, Econometrics, and the Death Penalty," in *Crime and Delinquency* 26 (Oct., 1980): 490-91.

19. Passell, Peter, and John B. Taylor, "The Deterrent Effect of Capital Punishment: Another View," in *American Economic Review* 67 (June, 1977): 449.

20. Between 1960-69 the murder rate increased by forty-four percent, with the largest proportion of this increase occurring between 1964-69, according to the *FBI Uniform Crime Reports 1969*, p. 6.

21. Yunker, James, "Is the Death Penalty a Deterrent to Homicide? Some Time Series Evidence," in *Journal of Behavorial Economics* 6 (Summer/Winter, 1977): 65.

22. Passell, Peter, "The Deterrent Effect of the Death Penalty: A Statistical Test," in *Stanford Law Review* 28 (Nov., 1975): 80.

23. *Ibid.*, p. 79.
24. Forst, Brian E., "The Deterrent Effect of Capital Punishment: A Cross-State Analysis of the 1960s," in *Minnesota Law Review* 61 (May, 1977): 784.
25. *Ibid.*, p. 755.
26. *Ibid.*, p. 762-63.
27. Ehrlich, Isaac, "Capital Punishment and Deterrence: Some Further Thoughts and Additional Evidence," in *Journal of Political Economy* 85 (Aug., 1977): 779.
28. Cloninger, Dale O., "Deterrence and the Death Penalty: A Cross-Sectional Analysis," in *Journal of Behavioral Economics* 6 (Summer/Winter, 1977): 87-106.
29. Boyes, William J., and Lee R. McPheters, "Capital Punishment As a Deterrent to Violent Crime: Cross Sectional Evidence," in *Journal of Behavioral Economics* 6 (Summer/Winter, 1977): 83.
30. *Ibid.*
31. Gibbs, Jack, "A Critique of the Scientific Literature on Capital Punishment and Deterrence," in *Journal of Behavioral Economics* 6 (Summer/Winter, 1977): 305-06.
32. Decker, Scott H., and Carol W. Kohfeld, *An Empirical Analysis of the Effect of the Death Penalty in Missouri*, p. 8.
33. Futch, Clifford, in *Corrections Magazine* 2 (Sept., 1975): 39.
34. Agnew, Spiro T. (then Vice President of the U.S.), remarks made in 1971 to the New York Times News Service, exact citation and date unknown.
35. Badinter, Robert, "Remarks on the Death Penalty Before Amnesty International USA," Amnesty International, Inc., New York, Jan. 25, 1983.
36. Wills, Gary, writing in a column entitled, "There Is No Way to Counter Death But with Life," published by the District of Columbia Coalition Against the Death Penalty, date unknown.
37. Trott, Stephen S., Asst. Attorney General, Criminal Division, U.S. Dept. of Justice, speaking to the U.S. House of Representatives Judiciary Committee, March 7, 1985.

CHAPTER V

1. Wang Jingrong, Chinese Ministry of Public Security, *Washington Post* (November 15, 1984): A33.
2. Camus, Albert, *Essay Against Capital Punishment*, 1957.
3. Goodman, Ellen, *Miami Herald* (Mar. 20, 1984). UPI wire story.
4. Gettinger, S. H., *Sentenced to Die* (New York: Macmillan Publishing Co., 1979), p. 87.
5. Brasfield, Philip, with Jeffrey M. Elliot, *Deathman Pass Me By: Two Years on Death Row* (San Bernardino, CA: The Borgo Press, 1983), p. 7.
6. *Ibid.*, p. 74.
7. Bruck, David, Attorney speaking before hearings of the U.S. House of Representatives Subcommittee on Criminal Justice, Nov. 7, 1985.
8. Rockefeller, Winthrop, in *Time Magazine* (Dec. 8, 1986): 45.
9. Carruthers, Garey, *Ibid.*, p. 45.
10. Anaya, Toney (Gov. of New Mexico), in *The New York Times* (Nov. 28, 1986): 18.
11. Gray vs. Lucas, 710 F 2nd 1048 (5th Cir) Cert denied 104 S.Ct. 211 (1983), p. 1058 *Federal Reporter, 2d Ser.*
12. *Ibid.*, p. 1059.

13. *Ibid.*, p. 1059.
14. *Ibid.*, p. 519-521.
15. Ibsen, Henrik, *An Enemy of the People* (1882), Act. IV.
16. *Ibid.*, Act V.

CHAPTER VI

1.   Sellin, Thorsten, "Capital Punishment," in *Federal Probation* (Sept., 1961): 10.
2.   428 U.S. 153 (1976).
3.   428 U.S. 280 (1976).
4.   Proffitt v. Florida, 428 U.S. 242 (1976); Jurek v. Texas, 428 U.S. 262 (1976); Roberts v. Louisiana, 428 U.S. 325 (1976).
5.   Wolfgang, Marvin E., and Marc Riedel, "Race, Judicial Discretion, and the Death Penalty," in *The Annals* 407 (May, 1973): 123.
6.   433 U.S. 584 (1977).
7.   Bowers, William J., and Glenn L. Pierce, "Arbitrariness and Discrimination Under Post-*Furman* Capital Statutes," in *Crime and Delinquency* 26 (Oct., 1980): 576.
8.   Johnson, Guy B., "The Negro and Crime," in *The Annals* 217 (Sept., 1941): 98.
9.   Bowers and Pierce, p. 576-579.
10   Mangum, Charles, *The Legal Status of the Negro* (Chapel Hill, NC: University of North Carolina Press, 1940).
11. Wolfgang, Marvin, Arlene Kelly, and Hans Nolde, "Comparison of Executed and Commuted Among Admissions to Death Row," cited by Bowers and Pierce, p. 581.
12. Wolfgang, Marvin, and Marc Riedel, "Race, Judicial Discretion, and the Death Penalty," p. 130.
13. *Ibid.*, p. 132.
14. Wolfgang, Marvin, and Marc Riedel, "Rape, Race, and the Death Penalty in Georgia," in *American Journal of Orthopsychiatry* 45 (July, 1975): 667.
15. Judson, Charles J., *et al.*, "A Study of the California Penalty Jury in First-Degree-Murder Cases," in *Stanford Law Review* 21 (June, 1969 [special issue]): 1377-79.
16. *Ibid.*, p. 1421-22.
17. Riedel, Marc, "Discrimination in the Imposition of the Death Penalty: A Comparison of the Characteristics of Offenders Sentenced Pre-*Furman* and Post-*Furman*," in *Temple Law Quarterly* 49 (Winter, 1976): 276-79.
18. *Ibid.*, p. 280-81.
19. *Ibid.*, p. 282.
20. The statutes of Florida, Georgia, and Texas were specifically upheld by the Supreme Court. The addition of Ohio brought the representation in the sample of post-*Furman* death ssentences to approximately seventy percent. The Ohio statute was subsequently held to be unconstitutional in Lockett v. Ohio (438 U.S. 586 [1978]), and, therefore, Bowers and Pierce did not use the data from this state for any further analyses.
21. Bowers and Pierce, p. 598.
22. *Ibid.*, p. 630.
23. *Ibid.*, p. 620.
24. *Ibid.*, p. 623.
25. *Ibid.*, p. 624-25.
26. *Ibid.*, p. 629.

27. *Ibid.*, p. 629-30.

28. CBC Amici Curiae Brief, U.S. Supreme Court, October Term 1986, p. 19.

29. Cotton, Orandra, and Sherille Ismail, CBCF Staff, *Point of View* paper, citing *New Republic*.

30. Brennan, Justice William, McCleskey v. Kemp.

31. Wicker, Tom, "Death and Disparity," in *The New York Times* (May 16, 1987).

32. *Ibid.*

33. Donne, John, *Devotions* (1623), XVII.

34. Douglas, Justice William O., Furman v. Georgia, 408 U.S. 238 (1972).

35. St. James, Warren, *NAACP: Triumphs of a Pressure Group, 1909-1980* (Smithtown, NY: Exposition Press, 1985), p. 29.

36. Ploski, Harry A., ed., *The Negro Almanac* (published annually); and *The Crisis* (official publication of the NAACP) (1976): 29.

37. Trott, Stephen S., Asst. Attorney General, Criminal Division, U.S. Dept. of Justice, speaking before the U.S. House of Representatives Subcommittee on Criminal Justice, Nov. 7, 1985, p. 9.

38. Fosdick, Raymond, *American Police System* (orig. 1920; reprinted: Montclair, NJ: Patterson Smith, 1972), p. 72.

39. Sargent, Edward D., in *The Washington Post* (Mar. 2, 1986): C-1.

40. Powdermaker, Hortense, *After Freedom* (New York: Viking Press, 1939), p. 173.

41. Bruck, David, "Decisions of Death," in *The New Republic* (Dec. 12, 1983): 19.

42. Bond, Julian, State Senator of Georgia, writing in a column which appeared in the *St. Louis American* (date unknown).

43. Green, Paul, a Chapel Hill, NC, playwright.

44. Lawes, Lewis E., Warden of Sing Sing Prison, New York.

45. Frankfurter, Justice Felix, Irvin v. Dowd, 730.

46. Marshall, Justice Thurgood, speaking at the Judicial Conference of the U.S. Court of Appeals for the Second Circuit, Sept. 6, 1985.

47. *ABA Journal* (Jan. 1, 1987): 58.

48. Frankfurter, Justice Felix, Wilkerson v. McCarthy, 363 U.S. 53 and 65, S. Ct. 413 and 419, 93 L. Ed. 497 and 506 (1949).

49. "Death Row in America," in *Corrections Magazine* (Sept., 1976): 42.

50. *St. Louis Post-Dispatch* (Jan. 18, 1985): 2B.

51. Sansing, John, "Getting Revenge or Is It Justice?" in *The Washingtonian* (Feb., 1983).

52. Powell, Justice Lewis, Booth v. Maryland, June 15, 1987, p. 12.

53. Simon, Ruth, "25 Juveniles on Death Row; Should Age Barriers Be Set?" in *The National Law Journal* (Aug. 8, 1983): 21. Reproduced with permission.

54. *Numbers* 23:23, Bible.

55. Graham, Robert, Governor of Florida, *Sojourners* (July, 1979).

56. *Washington Post* (Feb. 12, 1984): editorial.

57. Jefferson, Thomas, source unknown.

58. Jefferson, Thomas, "To the Republican Citizens of Washington County, Maryland" (Mar. 31, 1809).

BIBLIOGRAPHY

"American Catholic Bishops Detail Opposition to Capital Punishment." *Washington Post* (Nov. 14, 1983).

Anaya, Toney. *New York Times* (Nov. 28, 1986).

"Antiabortionists Oppose Adding Other Causes to Pro-Life Banner." *Washington Post* (Jan. 30, 1984).

Badinter, Robert. "Remarks on the Death Penalty Before Amnesty International USA." New York: Amnesty International Inc., 1983.

Baldus, David C., and James W. L. Cole. "A Comparison of the Work of Thorsten Sellin and Isaac Ehrlich on the Deterrent Effect of Capital Punishment." *Yale Law Journal* (Dec., 1975).

Bedau, Hugo. *The Case Against the Death Penalty.* New York: ACLU, 1984.

Bedau, Hugo. *The Death Penalty in America.* Garden City, NY: Anchor Books, 1964.

Berns, Walter. *For Capital Punishment.* New York: Basic Books, 1979.

Blank, Rabbi Irvin M. Remarks before the House Subcommittee on Criminal Justice, Nov. 7, 1985.

Bond, Julian. A column in the *St. Louis American*, data unknown.

Bowers, William, and Glenn R. Pierce. "Arbitrariness and Discrimination Under Post-Furman Capital Statutes." *Crime and Delinquency* (Oct., 1980).

Boyes, William J., and Lee R. McPheters. "Capital Punishment As a Deterrent to Violent Crime: Cross Sectional Evidence." *Journal of Behavioral Economics* (Summer/Winter, 1977).

Brasfield, Philip, with Jeffrey M. Elliot. *Deathman Pass Me By: Two Years on Death Row.* San Bernardino, CA: The Borgo Press, 1983.

Bruck, David. "Decisions of Death." *New Republic* (Dec. 12, 1983).

Bruck, David. Remarks made before the House Subcommittee on Criminal Justice, Nov. 7, 1985.

Camus, Albert. *Essay Against Capital Punishment.* 1957.

Camus, Albert. "Reflections on the Guillotine." *Evergreen Review* (1957).

Carruthers, Garey. *Time* (Dec. 8, 1986).

"Catholics Split on Life Issues." *St. Louis Post-Dispatch* (Mar. 17, 1984).

Chambliss, W. "Types of Deviance and the Effectiveness of Legal Sanctions." *Wisconsin Law Review* (Summer, 1967).

Chavez, Rev. Guillermo. Remarks before the House Subcommittee on Criminal Justice, Nov. 7, 1985.

Cloninger, Dale O. "Deterrence and the Death Penalty: A Cross-Sectional Analysis." *Journal of Behavioral Economics* (Summer/Winter, 1977).

Cotton, Orandra, and Sherille Ismail. *Point of View* paper. CBCF, date unknown.

Craveri, Marcello. *The Life of Jesus.* New York: Echo Press, 1989.

Dante Alighieri. *Inferno*, Canto III.

"Death Row in America." *Corrections Magazine* (Sept., 1976).

Decker, Scott H., and Carol W. Kohfeld. *An Empirical Analysis of the Effect of the Death Penalty in Missouri.*

Drinan, Rev. Robert E. "The Catholic Bishops of United States Oppose Capital Punishment." *Congressional Record* (Nov. 19, 1980).

172

Ehrlich, Isaac. "Capital Punishment and Deterrence: Some Further Thoughts and Additional Evidence." *Journal of Political Economy* (Aug., 1977).

Ehrlich, Isaac. "Deterrence: Evidence and Inference." *Yale Law Journal* (Dec., 1975).

Ehrlich, Isaac. "The Deterrent Effect of Capital Punishment: A Question of Life and Death." *American Economic Review* (June, 1975).

"An Eye for an Eye." *Time* (Jan. 24, 1983).

Forst, Brian E. "The Deterrent Effect of Capital Punishment: A Cross-State Analysis of the 1960s." *Minnesota Law Review* (May, 1977).

Fosdick, Raymond. *American Police System*. Montclair, NJ: Patterson Smith, 1972.

Futch, Clifford. *Corrections Magazine* (Sept., 1975).

Gekas, Rep. George (R-Pa.). "Dear Colleague Letter" (June 10, 1985).

Gettinger, S. H. *Sentenced to Die*. New York: Macmillan Pub. Co., 1979.

Gibbs, Jack. "A Critique of the Scientific Literature on Capital Punishment and Deterrence." *Journal of Behavioral Economics* (Summer/ Winter, 1977).

Goodman, Ellen. Column in *Miami Herald* (Mar. 20, 1984). Also issued as a UPI wire story on the same date.

Goodman, Walter. "Religious Alliance Against Execution Grows." *New York Times* (Dec. 7, 1983).

Graham, Gov. Robert. *Sojourners* (July, 1979).

Ibsen, Henrik. *An Enemy of the People*. 1882.

Jefferson, Thomas. *Declaration of Independence* (July 5, 1776).

Jefferson, Thomas. "To the Republican Citizens of Washington County, Maryland." March 31, 1809.

Johnson, Guy B. "The Negro and Crime." *Annals* (Sept., 1941).

John Paul II, Pope, quoted in *Washington Post* (Jan. 16, 1983).

Judson, Charles J., *et al.* "A Study of the California Penalty Jury in First-Degree-Murder Cases." *Stanford Law Review* (June, 1969).

Klein, Lawrence R., Brian Forst, and Victor Filatov. "The Deterrent Effect of Capital Punishment: An Assessment of the Estimates." Blumstein, Alfred *et al.*, eds. *Deterrence and Incapacitation: Estimating the Effects of Criminal Sanctions on Crime Rates*. Washington: National Academy of Sciences, 1978.

Knorr, Stephen J. "Deterrence and the Death Penalty: A Temporal Cross-Sectional Approach." *Journal of Criminal Law and Criminology* (Summer, 1979).

Mangum, Charles. *The Legal Status of the Negro*. Chapel Hill, NC: University of North Carolina Press, 1940.

Mathews, Jay. *Washington Post* (Jan. 18, 1983).

McGahey, Richard M. "Economic Theory, Econometrics, and the Death Penalty." *Crime and Delinquency* (Oct., 1980).

"No Indictment for Lynching of Sikeston Negro." *St. Louis Post-Dispatch* (Mar. 11, 1942).

Passell, Peter, and John B. Taylor. "The Deterrent Effect of Capital Punishment: Another View." *American Economic Review* (June, 1977).

Passell, Peter. "The Deterrent Effect of the Death Penalty: A Statistical Test." *Stanford Law Review* (Nov., 1975).

Peck, Jon K. "The Deterrent Value of Capital Punishment: Ehrlich and His Critics." *Yale Law Journal* (Jan., 1976).

Ploski, Harry A. *The Negro Almanac*. Annual.

"The Pope and the Death Penalty." *Newsweek* (Dec. 12, 1983).

Powdermaker, Hortense. *After Freedom*. New York: Viking Press, 1939.

Riedel, Marc. "Discrimination in the Imposition of the Death Penalty: A Comparison of the Characteristics of Offenders Sentenced Pre-Furman and Post-Furman." *Temple Law Quarterly* (Winter, 1976).

Rockefeller, Winthrop. *Time* (Dec. 8, 1986).

Sansing, John. "Getting Revenge or Is It Justice?" *Washingtonian* (Feb., 1983).

Santayana, George. *The Life of Reason.* 1905-06, volume 1.

Sargent, Edward D. *Washington Post* (Mar. 2, 1986).

Scheussler, Karl F. "The Deterrent Influence of the Death Penalty." *Annals* (Nov., 1952).

Sellin, Thorsten. "Capital Punishment." *Federal Probation* (Sept., 1961).

Sellin, Thorsten. *Capital Punishment.* New York: Harper & Row, 1967.

Sellin, Thorsten. *The Death Penalty.* Philadelphia: American Law Institute, 1959.

"Sikeston Inquiry Seeks to Identify Men in Lynching." *St. Louis Post-Dispatch* (Jan. 30, 1942).

Simon, Ruth. "25 Juveniles on Death Row: Should Age Barriers Be Set?" *National Law Journal* (Aug. 8, 1983).

St. James, Warren. *NAACP: Triumphs of a Pressure Group, 1909-1980.* Smithtown, NY: Exposition Press, 1985.

Trott, Stephen S. Remarks made before the House Judiciary Committee, Mar. 7, 1985.

Trott, Stephen S. Remarks made before the House Subcommittee on Criminal Justice, Nov. 7, 1985.

U.S. Federal Bureau of Investigation. *FBI Uniform Crime Reports 1969.* Washington: GPO, 1969.

Van den Haag, Ernest. "On Deterrence and the Death Penalty." *Journal of Criminal Law, Criminology, and Police Science* (June, 1969).

Wang Jingrong. *Washington Post* (Nov. 15, 1984).

Wicker, Tom. "Death and Disparity." *New York Times* (May 16, 1987).

Wills, Gary. "There Is No Way to Counter Death But with Life." Washington: District of Columbia Coalition Against the Death Penalty, n.d.

Wolfgang, Marvin E., and Marc Riedel. "Race, Judicial Discretion, and the Death Penalty." *Annals* (May, 1973).

Wolfgang, Marvin E., and Marc Riedel. "Rape, Race, and the Death Penalty in Georgia." *American Journal of Orthopsychiatry* (July, 1975).

Wolfgang, Marvin E., Arlene Kelly, and Hans Nolde. "Comparison of Executed and Commuted Among Admissions to Death Row." *Crime and Delinquency* (Oct., 1980).

Yunker, James. "Is the Death Penalty a Deterrent to Homicide? Some Time Series Evidence." *Journal of Behavioral Economics* (Summer/ Winter, 1977).

APPENDIX

Statistical Tables

TABLE A

Murder Circumstances/Motives 1986

	Number*	Percent
Felony Total	3,736	19.4%
Robbery	1,926	9.5%
Narcotics	751	3.9%
Sex Offenses	289	1.5%
Arson	193	1.0%
Other Felonies	655	3.4%
Suspected Felonies	385	2.0%
Argument Total	7,221	37.5%
Romantic Triangle	404	2.1%
Property/Money	462	2.4%
Other Arguments	6,335	32.9%
Miscellaneous Non-Felony Types	3,576	18.6%
Unknown	4,332	22.5%
Totals:	19,257	100.0%

*Estimates based on percentages supplied by the FBI. Number may not equal the percent of total due to rounding. Source: U.S. Dept. of Justice. Federal Bureau of Investigation. *Uniform Crime Reports, 1986.* Washington: Government Printing Office, 1987, p. 12.

TABLES B-C

Percentages of Black Population and Black Prison Population in Selected States

State	Population	Prisoners
California	7.7%	35%
Florida	13.8%	49%
Georgia	26.8%	59%
North Carolina	22.4%	54%
Ohio	10.0%	50%
Texas	12.0%	43%

Source: Figures are estimates prepared by CRS. Figures are based on population counts found in: U.S. Dept. of Commerce. Bureau of the Census. *General Population Characteristics, 1980*. Washington: U.S. Government Printing Office, 1983, Table 61; and U.S. Dept. of Justice. Bureau of Justice Statistics. *Prisoners in State and Federal Institutions on Dec. 31, 1983*. Washington: GPO, 1985.

TABLE D

Probability of Receiving the Death Sentence for Criminal Homicide, by Race of Offender and Victim

Offender/Victim Race Combinations	Estimated Number of Offenders	Persons Sentenced to Death	Overall Probability of Death
Florida			
Black kills white	240	53	.221
White kills white	1,768	82	.046
Black kills black	1,922	12	.006
White kills black	80	0	.000
Georgia			
Black kills white	258	43	.167
White kills white	1,006	42	.042
Black kills black	2,458	12	.005
White kills black	71	2	.028
Texas			
Black kills white	344	30	.087
White kills white	3,616	56	.015
Black kills black	2,597	2	.001
White kills black	143	1	.007
Ohio			
Black kills white	173	44	.254
White kills white	803	37	.046
Black kills black	1,170	20	.017
White kills black	47	0	.000

Source: William J. Bowers and Glenn L. Pierce. "Arbitrariness and Discrimination under Post-*Furman* Capital Statutes," in *Crime and Delinquency* 26 (Oct., 1980): 594.

TABLE E

Probability of Receiving the Death Sentence in Florida and Georgia for Criminal Homicide, by Judicial Circuits/Counties, Grouped Regionally

Regional Grouping of Judicial Circuits/ Counties	Number of Homi- cides	Number of Death Sentences	Overall Probability of Death Sentence
Florida			
Panhandle	415	20	.048
North	976	34	.035
Central	1,526	54	.035
South	1,927	39	.020
Georgia			
North	289	2	.007
Central	1,011	45	.045
Atlanta	1,133	7	.006
Southwest	985	23	.023
Southeast	837	22	.026

Source: William J. Bowers and Glenn L. Pierce. "Arbitrariness and Discrimination under Post-*Furman* Capital Statutes," in *Crime and Delinquency* 26 (Oct., 1980): 603.

TABLE I

Murder Rate Per 100,000 Population

States with Death Penalty

State	Murders	Rate
Alabama	396	9.8
Arizona	254	8.0
Arkansas	187	7.9
California	2,770	10.5
Colorado	189	5.8
Connecticut	120	3.8
Delaware	30	4.8
Florida	1,296	11.4
Georgia	620	10.4
Idaho	22	2.2
Illinois	927	8.0
Indiana	319	5.8
Kentucky	256	6.9
Louisiana	487	10.9
Maryland	348	7.9
Mississippi	276	10.6
Missouri	409	8.1
Montana	48	5.8
Nebraska	47	2.9
Nevada	96	10.3
New Hamp.	21	2.1
New Jersey	407	5.4
New Mexico	158	10.9
No. Carolina	520	8.3
Ohio	554	5.2
Oklahoma	254	7.7
Oregon	125	4.7
Pennsylvania	550	4.6
Rhode Island	35	3.6

South Carolina	304	9.1
South Dakota	13	1.8
Tennessee	429	9.0
Texas	2,132	13.0
Utah	50	3.0
Vermont	18	3.4
Virginia	405	7.1
Washington	231	5.2
Wyoming	22	4.3

States with No Death Penalty

State	Murders	Rate
Alaska	51	9.8
Hawaii	43	4.1
Iowa	55	1.9
Kansas	121	4.9
Maine	28	2.4
Massachusetts	202	3.5
Michigan	1,018	11.2
Minnesota	88	2.1
New York	1,683	9.5
North Dakota	7	1.0
West Virginia	73	3.8
Wisconsin	135	2.8

Note: Table prepared by CRS. Source of population and murder data is "Table 5: Index of Crime by State, 1985," in *Uniform Crime Reports for the United States. 1985.* Information on states with death penalty statutes obtained from: U.S. Dept. of Justice. Bureau of Justice Statistics. *Capital Punishment, 1985.*

Murder Rate Averages

| States with Death Penalty: | 6.85 |
| States with No Death Penalty: | 4.75 |

TABLE II

Average Murder Rate Per 100,000 Population
In Each Federal Judicial Circuit

Federal Circuit	# States	Rate	Population
First Circuit			
No Death	3	3.2	7,954,000
Death Penalty	1	2.1	998,000
Totals	4	2.6	8,952,000
Second Circuit			
No Death	1	9.5	17,783,000
Death Penalty	2	3.6	3,709,000
Totals	3	6.5	21,492,000
Third Circuit			
No Death	0	0	0
Death Penalty	3	4.9	20,037,000
Totals	3	4.9	20,037,000
Fourth Circuit			
No Death	1	3.8	1,936,000
Death Penalty	4	8.1	19,700,000
Totals	5	5.9	21,636,000
Fifth Circuit			
No Death	0	0	0
Death Penalty	3	11.5	23,464,000
Totals	3	11.5	23,464,000
Sixth Circuit			
No Death	1	11.2	9,088,000
Death Penalty	3	7.0	19,762,000
Totals	4	9.1	28,850,000
Seventh Circuit			
No Death	1	2.8	4,775,000
Death Penalty	2	6.9	17,034,000
Totals	3	4.8	21,808,000
Eighth Circuit			
No Death	3	1.6	7,762,000

Death Penalty	4	5.2	9,702,000
Totals	7	3.4	25,226,000
Ninth Circuit			
No Death	2	6.9	1,575,000
Death Penalty	7	6.3	38,510,000
Totals	9	6.8	40,085,000
Tenth Circuit			
No Death	1	4.9	2,450,000
Death Penalty	5	6.3	10,136,000
Totals	6	5.6	12,586,000
Eleventh Circ.			
No Death	0	0	0
Death Penalty	3	10.5	21,363,000
Totals	3	10.5	21,363,000

Note: Prepared by CRS. Source: Data are based on figures appearing in the *Uniform Crime Reports for the United States, 1985*. States in each Judicial Circuit are: First: Maine, Massachusetts, New Hampshire, Rhode Island; Second: Connecticut, New York, Vermont; Third: Delaware, New Jersey, Pennsylvania; Fourth: Maryland, North Carolina, South Carolina, Virginia, West Virginia; Fifth: Louisiana, Mississippi, Texas; Sixth: Kentucky, Michigan, Ohio, Tennessee; Seventh: Illinois, Indiana, Wisconsin; Eighth: Arkansas, Iowa, Minnesota, Missouri, Nebraska, North Dakota, South Dakota; Ninth: Alaska, California, Hawaii, Idaho, Montana, Nevada, Oregon, Washington; Tenth: Colorado, Kansas, New Mexico, Oklahoma, Utah, Wyoming; Eleventh: Alabama, Florida, Georgia.

TABLE III

Estimated Murder Rates for Selected States with Death Penalty Statutes Repealed or Invalidated in the 1970s

Year	CO	KS	MA	MO	NJ	NM	OH	SD	WA
1971	6.5	5.1	3.8	8.9	5.8	11.6	7.5	1.2	3.8
1972	8.3	4.0	3.7	8.3[1]	6.5[1]	11.1	7.5	1.2	4.2
1973	7.9	6.0[1]	4.4	9.0	7.4	11.3	7.3	3.8	4.0[1]
1974	6.0	6.9	4.4	9.8	6.7	11.3	8.9	2.1	5.1
1975	7.4	5.4	4.1[1]	10.6[2]	6.8	13.3	8.1	3.7	5.7
1976	6.8	4.5	3.3	9.3	5.3	9.7[1]	7.4	1.7	4.3[2]
1977	6.3	6.6	3.1	9.6	5.6	8.8	7.8	2.0[1]	4.3
1978	7.3[1]	5.7	3.7	10.4	5.4	10.2	6.9[1]	1.9	4.6
1979	5.8[2]	5.5	3.7[2]	11.2	6.6	12.4[2]	8.1	2.0[2]	4.8

Source: FBI *Uniform Crime Reports*, 1971-1979.
1 = Year death penalty was repealed or invalidated.
2 = Year death penalty was reinstated.

TABLE IV

Number of Individuals Under Sentence of Death, by Race, 1973-1979

State	Whites							Blacks						
	73	74	75	76	77	78	79	73	74	75	76	77	78	79
AL	1	0	0	2	11	19	18	1	0	0	2	8	22	25
AZ	3	5	8	14	14	7	19	0	3	4	2	4	1	3
AR	0	1	3	4	5	7	7	0	0	1	2	2	4	5
CA	18	14	22	43	32	6	18	11	7	16	25	22	3	5
CO	0	0	1	1	3	0	0	0	0	0	2	2	0	0
DE	0	0	2	0	0	1	1	0	0	1	0	0	0	0
FL	5	18	32	49	56	71	79	9	18	30	32	40	50	59
GA	7	13	10	16	24	27	33	3	7	15	18	25	30	38
ID	0	0	0	2	0	0	1	0	0	0	0	0	0	0
IL	9	3	1	0	0	4	10	2	1	2	0	1	1	9
IN	3	1	4	5	0	0	0	2	1	3	2	0	2	3
KY	3	3	5	3	0	2	2	2	1	0	0	0	1	1
LA	2	2	5	3	0	0	1	9	17	29	27	0	1	1
MD	0	0	0	0	0	0	1	4	3	2	0	0	0	0
MA	11	5	4	0	0	0	0	14	12	5	0	0	0	0
MS	0	0	3	0	2	3	4	1	3	13	1	6	7	7
MO	1	0	0	0	0	0	1	1	1	0	0	0	0	1
MT	0	0	3	4	4	3	2	0	0	1	1	1	1	1
NE	0	0	1	4	4	6	6	0	0	1	1	0	2	2
NV	0	0	1	3	3	6	7	0	0	0	0	0	0	0
NM	0	7	6	0	0	0	0	0	0	0	0	0	0	0
NY	0	0	0	0	0	0	0	2	0	1	2	0	0	0
NC	6	21	30	0	0	4	4	15	39	68	0	0	1	4
OH	0	0	11	26	31	0	0	0	5	22	41	56	0	0
OK	0	5	14	0	4	12	21	0	2	12	0	1	4	4
OR	0	0	0	0	0	0	1	0	0	0	0	0	0	0
PA	4	4	4	3	0	0	2	3	2	1	3	0	0	2
RI	0	0	0	0	0	0	0	0	0	1	2	2	2	0
SC	0	0	8	0	2	3	7	0	0	5	0	2	4	1
TN	0	1	8	19	0	6	9	0	0	6	15	0	1	2
TX	0	6	20	34	43	62	75	0	3	11	19	22	38	42
UT	4	3	5	4	4	4	5	0	2	2	2	2	2	2
VA	2	2	1	0	0	2	4	1	2	2	0	1	4	4
WA	0	0	0	0	2	6	5	0	0	0	0	0	0	0
WY	0	2	2	3	0	0	1	0	2	2	2	0	0	0

Totals

Year	Whites	Blacks	Totals
1973	79	80	159
1974	116	131	247
1975	214	256	470
1976	242	201	443
1977	244	197	441
1978	261	181	442
1979	344	221	565

Note: Tables prepared by CRS. Source: U.S. Dept. of Justice. *Capital Punishment*, 1973-1979. In 1976 this series altered the way it counted inmates sentenced to death; those sentenced to death under statutes later found to be unconstitutional were now removed from the count as of the date of the relevant decision, rather than the date of specific application of the finding to the individual. Not included in these tables are the handful of individuals in "other racial" categories.

TABLE V

Number of Individuals Receiving Sentence of Death, by Race, 1973-1979

State	Whites							Blacks						
	73	74	75	76	77	78	79	73	74	75	76	77	78	79
AL	0	0	0	2	9	8	4	1	0	0	1	6	12	6
AZ	0	5	4	7	2	8	14	0	3	1	0	2	2	2
AR	0	1	2	1	1	2	0	0	0	1	1	1	2	2
CA	0	7	15	23	0	6	0	0	1	13	9	0	1	0
CO	0	0	1	1	2	0	13	0	0	0	2	0	1	5
DE	0	0	2	3	0	1	0	0	0	1	4	0	0	0
FL	5	13	12	22	14	17	11	7	11	16	7	10	14	12
GA	0	7	1	4	4	3	4	0	4	8	5	6	2	8
ID	0	0	0	2	0	0	1	0	0	0	0	0	0	0
IL	0	0	0	0	0	4	6	0	0	2	0	1	0	8
IN	0	0	4	1	0	0	0	0	1	2	0	1	0	8
KY	0	0	3	0	0	2	0	0	0	0	0	0	1	0
LA	1	0	3	0	0	0	0	0	4	5	0	0	1	0
MD	0	0	0	0	0	0	1	0	0	0	1	0	0	0
MA	0	0	1	0	0	0	0	4	1	0	0	0	0	0
MS	0	0	3	0	2	1	1	0	3	11	5	5	1	0
MO	0	0	0	0	0	0	1	0	0	0	0	0	0	1
MT	0	0	0	1	0	0	0	0	0	0	0	0	0	0
NE	0	0	1	3	0	2	1	0	0	1	0	0	2	0
NV	0	0	1	2	1	4	3	0	0	0	0	0	0	0
NM	0	7	3	3	0	0	0	0	0	0	0	0	0	0
NY	0	0	0	0	0	0	0	0	0	1	1	0	0	0
NC	6	12	12	8	1	4	3	15	17	33	11	0	1	4
OH	0	0	11	1	15	9	4	0	5	17	19	16	9	0
OK	0	5	10	6	4	8	9	0	2	10	2	1	4	0
OR	0	0	0	0	0	0	1	0	0	0	0	0	0	0
PA	1	0	1	1	2	0	2	0	0	0	4	6	0	2
RI	0	0	0	0	0	0	0	0	0	1	1	0	0	0
SC	0	0	8	8	2	1	4	0	0	5	5	2	2	1
TN	0	1	7	8	0	6	3	0	0	6	4	0	1	0
TX	0	7	13	12	12	21	11	0	3	6	4	4	12	6
UT	1	0	3	1	1	0	1	0	2	0	0	0	0	0
VA	0	0	0	1	0	2	2	0	1	0	2	1	3	1
WA	0	0	0	0	2	4	1	0	0	0	0	0	0	0
WY	0	2	0	1	0	0	1	0	2	0	0	0	0	0

Totals

Year	Whites	Blacks	Totals
1973	14	27	41
1974	67	60	127
1975	121	140	261
1976	136	88	224
1977	68	62	130
1978	108	73	181
1979	98	59	157

Note: Tables prepared by CRS. Source: U.S. Dept. of Justice. *Capital Punishment*, 1973-1979. In 1976 this series altered the way it counted inmates sentenced to death; those sentenced to death under statutes later found to be unconstitutional were now removed from the count as of the date of the relevant decision, rather than the date of specific application of the finding to the individual. Not included in these tables are the handful of individuals in "other racial" categories.

TABLE VI

Prisoners Executed Under Civil Authority in the United States By Race and Offenses—Regions and States (1930-1979)

Key Codes: T=Totals, All Races; 1=All Offenses; 2=Murder;
3=Rape; 4=Armed Robbery; 5=Kidnapping; 6=Other Felonies
N/E=Northeast; N/C=North Central; So.=South

Region/State		Whites						Blacks					
R/S	T	1	2	3	4	5	6	1	2	3	4	5	6
N/E	608	424	422	0	0	2	0	177	177	0	0	0	0
ME	0	0	0	0	0	0	0	0	0	0	0	0	0
NH	1	1	1	0	0	0	0	0	0	0	0	0	0
VT	4	4	4	0	0	0	0	0	0	0	0	0	0
MA	27	25	25	0	0	0	0	2	2	0	0	0	0
RI	0	0	0	0	0	0	0	0	0	0	0	0	0
CT	21	18	18	0	0	0	0	3	3	0	0	0	0
NY	329	234	232	0	0	2	0	90	90	0	0	0	0
NJ	74	47	47	0	0	0	0	25	25	0	0	0	0
PA	152	95	95	0	0	0	0	57	57	0	0	0	0
N/C	403	257	254	3	0	0	0	144	137	7	0	0	0
OH	172	104	104	0	0	0	0	67	67	0	0	0	0
IN	41	31	31	0	0	0	0	10	10	0	0	0	0
IL	90	59	59	0	0	0	0	31	31	0	0	0	0
MI	0	0	0	0	0	0	0	0	0	0	0	0	0
WI	0	0	0	0	0	0	0	0	0	0	0	0	0
MN	0	0	0	0	0	0	0	0	0	0	0	0	0
IA	18	18	18	0	0	0	0	0	0	0	0	0	0
MO	62	29	26	3	0	0	0	33	26	7	0	0	0
ND	0	0	0	0	0	0	0	0	0	0	0	0	0
SD	1	1	1	0	0	0	0	0	0	0	0	0	0
NE	4	3	3	0	0	0	0	0	0	0	0	0	0
KS	15	12	12	0	0	0	0	3	3	0	0	0	0
So.	2307	638	586	43	4	5	0	1659	1231	398	19	0	11
DE	12	5	4	1	0	0	0	7	4	3	0	0	0
MD	68	13	7	6	0	0	0	55	37	18	0	0	0
DC	40	3	3	0	0	0	0	37	34	3	0	0	0
VA	92	17	17	0	0	0	0	75	54	21	0	0	0
WV	40	31	28	0	0	3	0	9	8	1	0	0	0
NC	263	59	55	4	0	0	0	199	149	41	0	0	9
SC	162	35	30	5	0	0	0	127	90	37	0	0	0
GA	366	68	65	3	0	0	0	298	234	58	6	0	0

To Kill or Not to Kill

FL	171	58	56	1	0	1	0	113	78	35	0	0	0
KY	103	51	47	1	3	0	0	52	41	9	2	0	0
TN	93	27	22	5	0	0	0	66	44	22	0	0	0
AL	135	28	26	2	0	0	0	107	80	20	5	0	2
MS	154	30	30	0	0	0	0	124	100	21	3	0	0
AR	118	27	25	2	0	0	0	90	73	17	0	0	0
LA	133	30	30	0	0	0	0	103	86	17	0	0	0
OK	60	42	40	0	1	1	0	15	11	4	0	0	0
TX	297	114	101	13	0	0	0	182	108	71	3	0	0
West	511	407	395	0	0	7	5	83	82	0	0	0	1
MT	6	4	4	0	0	0	0	2	2	0	0	0	0
ID	3	3	3	0	0	0	0	0	0	0	0	0	0
WY	7	6	6	0	0	0	0	1	1	0	0	0	0
CO	47	41	41	0	0	0	0	5	5	0	0	0	0
NM	8	6	6	0	0	0	0	2	2	0	0	0	0
AZ	38	28	28	0	0	0	0	10	10	0	0	0	0
UT	14	14	14	0	0	0	0	0	0	0	0	0	0
NV	30	28	28	0	0	0	0	2	2	0	0	0	0
WA	47	40	39	0	0	1	0	5	5	0	0	0	0
OR	19	16	16	0	0	0	0	3	3	0	0	0	1
CA	292	221	210	0	0	6	5	53	52	0	0	0	0
AK	0	0	0	0	0	0	0	0	0	0	0	0	0
HI	0	0	0	0	0	0	0	0	0	0	0	0	0
State	3829	1726	1657	46	4	14	5	2063	1627	405	19	0	12
Fed.	33	28	10	2	2	6	8	3	3	0	0	0	0
Total	3862	1754	1647	48	6	20	13	2066	1630	405	19	0	12

Note: The "other" federal executions were for sabotage (6) and espionage (2); the nine "others" in N.C. and Ala. were for burglary; the six "others" in Calif. were for assault committed by prisoners under life sentence. Alaska and Hawaii are included beginning Jan. 1, 1960. Source: U.S. Dept. of Justice. Bureau of Justice Statistics. *Capital Punishment, 1979*, p. 18. Other races not included.

TABLE VII

Number of Persons Under Sentence of Death, by Race, on May 1, 1987

State	Totals	White	Black
Alabama	83	30	53
Arizona	54	48	6
California	159	83	76
Colorado	1	1	0
Connecticut	0	0	0
Delaware	6	1	5
Florida	251	156	95
Georgia	107	57	50
Idaho	13	13	0
Illinois	95	33	62
Indiana	40	21	19
Kentucky	31	23	8
Louisiana	52	24	28
Maryland	19	4	15
Mississippi	47	23	24
Missouri	49	29	20
Montana	6	5	1
Nebraska	12	10	2
Nevada	36	24	12
New Hamp.	0	0	0
New Jersey	24	11	13
New Mexico	0	0	0
No. Carolina	58	22	36
Ohio	73	35	38
Oregon	2	2	0
Pennsylvania	82	34	48
So. Carolina	50	26	24
So. Dakota	0	0	0
Tennessee	57	39	18
Texas	202	109	93

To Kill or Not to Kill

Utah	7	3	4
Vermont	0	0	0
Virginia	35	17	18
Washington	6	5	1
Wyoming	3	3	0
Totals	1755	962	793

Note: Table prepared by CRS. Excludes other races. Source: National Criminal Justice Reference Service.

TABLE VIII
Sections A-G
(seven tables taken from the Bureau of Justice Statistics)

TABLE VIII-A

Profile of Capital Punishment Statutes in 1985

Jurisdiction/Capital Offenses

Fed.	Aircraft piracy
AL	Murder
AZ	First degree murder
AR	Aggravated murder; treason
CA	First degree murder with special circumstances
CO	First degree murder (includes felony murder); first degree kidnapping
CT	Murder
DE	First degree murder with statutory aggravating circumstances
FL	First degree murder
GA	Murder; treason; aircraft hijacking; kidnapping with bodily injury; armed robbery or rape in which victim dies
ID	First degree murder; aggravated kidnapping (except where the victim is released unharmed)
IL	Murder
IN	Murder
KY	Aggravated murder; kidnapping when victim is killed
LA	First degree murder
MD	First degree murder
MS	Capital murder; capital rape
MO	First degree murder
MT	Deliberate homicide; aggravated kidnapping resulting in death
NE	First degree murder
NV	First degree murder
NH	Contract murder; murder of a law enforcement officer or kidnap-

	ping victim
NJ	Kidnapping or purposeful murder or contract murder with aggravating circumstances
NM	First degree murder
NC	First degree murder
OH	Aggravated murder
OK	Murder
OR	Aggravated murder
PA	First degree murder
SC	Murder with statutory aggravating circumstances
SD	Murder; kidnapping with gross permanent physical injury to the victim
TN	First degree murder
TX	Murder of public safety officer, fireman, or correctional employee; murder during specified felonies or escapes; contract murder; multiple murders
UT	First degree murder; aggravated assault by prisoner sentenced for first degree felony where serious injury is caused
VT	Murder of police or correctional officer; kidnapping for ransom
VA	Capital murder
WA	Aggravated, premeditated first degree murder
WY	First degree murder

Source: U.S. Dept. of Justice. Bureau of Justice Statistics.

TABLE VIII-B

Method of Execution, by State, in 1985

Key: I=Lethal Injection; E=Electrocution; L=Lethal
gas; H=Hanging; F=Firing squad

State	I	E	L	H	F
Alabama		x			
Arizona			x		
Arkansas	x	x			
California			x		
Colorado			x		
Connecticut		x			
Delaware				x	
Florida		x			
Georgia		x			
Idaho	x				x
Illinois	x				
Indiana		x			
Kentucky		x			
Louisiana		x			
Maryland			x		
Mississippi	x		x		
Missouri			x		
Montana	x			x	
Nebraska		x			
Nevada	x				
New Hamp.				x	
New Jersey	x				
New Mexico	x				
No. Carolina	x		x		
Ohio		x			
Oklahoma	x				
Oregon	x				

State					
Pennsylvania		X			
So. Carolina		X			
So. Dakota	X				
Tennessee		X			
Texas	X				
Utah	X				X
Vermont		X			
Virginia		X			
Washington	X			X	
Wyoming	X		X		

Note: Several states authorize two methods of execution; Oklahoma also authorizes execution by electrocution or firing squad should lethal injection be found unconstitutional.
Source: U.S. Dept. of Justice. Bureau of Justice Statistics.

TABLE VIII-C

Minimum Age Authorized for Capital Punishment 1985

10 years: Indiana, Vermont

13 years: Georgia, Mississippi

14 years: Missouri, North Carolina

15 years: Arkansas, Louisiana, Virginia

16 years: Connecticut, Montana, Nevada

17 years: New Hampshire, Texas

18 years: California, Colorado, Illinois, Nebraska, New Jersey, New Mexico, Ohio, Oregon*, Washington

No age specified: Federal, Alabama, Arizona, Delaware, Florida, Idaho, Kentucky, Maryland, Oklahoma, Pennsylvania, South Carolina, South Dakota*, Tennessee, Utah, Wyoming

Source: U.S. Dept. of Justice. Bureau of Justice Statistics.
* = Adult status at trial required.

TABLE VIII-D

**Demographic Profile of Prisoners
Under Sentence of Death 1985**

Types	Yearend '85	'85 Additions	'85 Removals
Sex			
Male	98.9%	98.9%	97.1%
Female	1.1%	1.1%	2.9%
Race			
White	56.8%	58.6%	61.8%
Black	42.3%	40.7%	36.3%
Other	1.0%	0.7%	2.0%
Ethnicity			
Hispanic	6.2%	6.2%	5.9%
Non-Hispanic	93.8%	93.8%	94.1%
Age			
16-19	0.8%	4.4%	0
20-24	13.3%	26.4%	9.8%
25-29	26.9%	25.3%	30.4%
30-34	23.6%	19.8%	23.5%
35-39	16.3%	9.9%	13.7%
40-54	17.0%	12.1%	20.6%
55+	2.0%	2.2%	2.0%
Median age	31.9 yrs.	28.0 yrs.	32.1 yrs.
Education			
7th gr. or less	10.8%	10.8%	9.9%
8th grade	11.7%	11.1%	13.6%
9th-11th	35.6%	39.4%	34.6%
12th (h.s.)	32.4%	30.3%	33.3%
Any college	9.4%	8.4%	8.6%
Median educ.	10.5 yrs.	10.4 yrs.	10.5 yrs.
Marital status			
Married	32.6%	28.0%	37.1%
Divorced/sep.	21.2%	22.2%	14.4%

Widowed	2.3%	3.5%	4.1%
Never marr.	43.9%	46.3%	44.3%

Source: U.S. Dept. of Justice. Bureau of Justice Statistics. Educational status of 235 prisoners and marital status of 98 prisoners not reported. "Other" race category includes 11 American Indians and 5 Asians. The youngest person under sentence of death was 16 in 1985; the oldest was 74. 1,591 persons were under sentence of death at yearend 1985, reflecting 273 admissions and 102 deletions during that year.

TABLE VIII-E

Criminal History Profile of Prisoners Under Sentence of Death, by Race, in 1985

	Number under sentence			Percent under sentence		
	All	White	Black	All	White	Black
Prior felony?						
Yes	970	528	432	66.2%	62.2%	71.9%
No	496	321	169	33.8%	37.8%	28.1%
Unknown	125	54	71			
Prior homicide?						
Yes	116	48	67	9.0%	6.5%	12.6%
No	1170	693	464	91.0%	93.5%	87.4%
Unknown	305	162	141			
Legal status						
Charges pending	85	55	28	6.6%	7.4%	5.2%
Probation	70	48	21	5.4%	6.5%	3.9%
Parole	260	123	137	20.1%	16.5%	25.6%
Prison escapee	36	22	14	2.8%	3.0%	2.6%
Prison inmate	44	24	20	3.4%	3.2%	3.7%
Other status	21	11	9	1.6%	1.5%	1.7%
None	776	461	307	60.1%	62.0%	57.3%
Unknown	299	159	136			

Source: U.S. Dept. of Justice. Bureau of Justice Statistics. Percents are based on offenders for whom data were reported. Category "all" includes whites, Blacks, and other races.

TABLE VIII-F

Percentage of Those Under Sentence of Death
Executed or Receiving Other Disposition, 1977-1985

Race	Death sentences Total	Actually executed Number	Percent	Other dispositions Number	Percent
All races	2530	50	2.0%	889	35.1%
White	1441	33	2.3%	505	35.0%
Black	1066	17	1.6%	377	35.4%

Source: U.S. Dept. of Justice. Bureau of Justice Statistics. Includes all those under sentence of death between 1977-85; "other dispositions" include persons removed from sentence of death due to statutes being struck down on appeal, sentences/convictions vacated, or death other than by execution.

TABLE VIII-G

Elapsed Time Between Imposition of Death
Sentence and Execution, by Race, 1977-1985

Year	Number executed All	White	Black	Average elapsed time till execution All	White	Black
Total	50	33	17	72 mo.	68 mo.	79 mo.
1977-83	11	9	2	58 mo.	59 mo.	58 mo.
1984	21	13	8	79 mo.	76 mo.	84 mo.
1985	18	11	7	71 mo.	65 mo.	80 mo.

Source: U.S. Dept. of Justice. Bureau of Justice Statistics. The average elapsed time was measured from sentencing date, and ranged from 3-133 months.

INDEX

ABOUT THE AUTHOR

Congressman William L. Clay, Sr., was born April 30, 1931 at St. Louis, Missouri, the son of Irving and Luella (Hyatt) Clay. He and his eight brothers and sisters were raised in a tenement apartment with no indoor plumbing or hot water; by the age of thirteen he was working as a janitor in a clothing store to help support his family. By eighteen he was a salesman; through his savings and scholarships he was able to attend college, graduating (as one of four Blacks in a class of 1,100) from St. Louis University in 1953 with a B.A. in history and political science. Later that same year he married Carol Ann Johnson, by whom he has three children: Vickie (born 1954); William Lacy, Jr. (born 1956), and Michele (born 1958). Following college he was drafted into the army, where he organized his fellow Black soldiers to protest against the segregation of minority noncoms from certain base facilities. After returning to St. Louis, he challenged the white incumbent of the Twenty-Sixth Ward, and was elected a city alderman (in a major election upset) in 1959, and was re-elected in 1963. In 1960 Clay was arrested for daring to eat at a segregated restaurant in St. Louis, and was briefly imprisoned in 1963 for publicly protesting against the "white only" hiring policies of a local bank. In 1968 he was elected to Congress from the First District, beating five primary opponents and a strong Republican candidate, and has been easily re-elected ever since, with margins ranging up to 96% of the vote. As a Congressman, William L. Clay immediately made his mark by protesting against Richard Nixon's civil rights policies, against the Vietnam War, and by founding the Congressional Black Caucus in 1971. He currently serves on the Committee on Education and Labor and the Committee on House Administration; he acts as Chair of the Subcommittees on Labor-Management Relations and the Subcommittee on Libraries and Memorials (which oversees the Library of Congress). He is the ranking Democrat on the Committee on the Post Office and Civil Service. Clay was the House sponsor of revisions in the pension law in the Tax Reform Act of 1986, and has also sponsored legislation for parental and medical leaves, for mandatory notification of plant closings, and for the protection of unions' negotiating rights. This is his first published book.